PLEASE TURN OUT THE NORTHERN LIGHTS WHEN YOU LEAVE

Barry H. Maughan

Illustrated with photographs and a route map

 www.trafford.com

North America & international
toll-free: 1 888 232 4444 (USA & Canada)
phone: 250 383 6864 ♦ fax: 812 355 4082

ABOUT THE AUTHOR...

BARRY MAUGHAN'S been a writer, journalist and international broadcaster for more than 30 years. So he's a past master at separating the unusual and the offbeat from the obvious and mundane. And he's not averse to injecting his own brand of humor as well.

Suzanne has shared her husband's wanderlust and joy in exploring new and interesting places throughout their 44 years of married life. Stops along the way have included assignments in Ethiopia and New Zealand.

In Ethiopia, Barry worked as a radio broadcaster and reporter for the Christian broadcasting station, Radio Voice of the Gospel. At the same time, he was a freelance correspondent and reporter for several international news organizations, including *The Financial Times of London, United Press International, the Voice of America, Radio New Zealand* and *To The Point* magazine.

More recently, Barry has turned his talents to writing articles for the *Escapees* magazine.

Since their retirement, Barry and his wife have spent a great deal of time traveling full time aboard Bridget, their large fully-equipped truck camper. They weren't accustomed to such luxurious living when, in the late 1960s, they began their caravanning experience by driving their Volkswagen camper van throughout Europe and ultimately overland from Alexandria, Egypt, to Cape Town, South Africa. In April, 2007, they wrapped up a year long circumnavigation of Australia—a journey that took them more than 16,000 miles through Barry's homeland in a 1995 Winnebago Mitsubishi Canter motorhome.

And don't let that "n" on the end of the Maughan surname fool you. Barry's a distant relative of the acclaimed British author, W. Somerset Maugham. But as Barry puts it, "Willie wouldn't have known me from a bar of soap!"

Barry is a graduate of the Cambridge School of Radio/TV Broadcasting in Boston and holds a B.A. in Journalism/Advertising from Boston University and an M.A. in Journalism/Management from Oklahoma State University.

ACKNOWLEDGMENTS

I OWE so many people so much it's hard to know where to start. This has been a project a long time in the works, as it's based on a trip to the Pacific Northwest in 2001. So to my dear wife, Suzanne, go my deepest thanks for keeping me motivated and never accepting any of my creative excuses for abandoning the effort.

My sincerest appreciation also goes to my children, Kevin and Angeline, and their spouses, Maureen and Ken, for never once rolling their eyes in disbelief at the number of times I told them my book was "nearly" completed.

Every writer needs a highly skilled editor and I certainly have mine in Fritzi Depew. Apart from being a dear friend of many years standing, Fritzi is a strict grammarian and a serious student of the complexities of the English language. What's more, she's one of the few people I know who can spot a dangling participle at thirty paces!

In addition, my deepest thanks to proof reader extraordinaire, Ursula Nebiker, for her patient, painstaking scrutiny of my every word.

And to all my friends who offered their advice, encouragement and support, my heartfelt gratitude also goes out to you.

DEDICATION

Dedicated to fellow travelers with wanderlust in
their soul and an incurable case of "hitch itch."

PREFACE

THINK THERE are no new interesting stories to be told about traveling through Alaska, Yukon, Northwest Territories and British Columbia? Well, think again!

Here's your opportunity to join Barry and Suzanne Maughan as they poke around the Pacific Northwest looking for the offbeat and unusual and generally finding both. While some of the superficialities may have changed since 2001, the country of the Pacific Northwest has retained much of its wild, untamed flavor, as have many of the characters still living there.

So come on along with the Maughans and get ready to expect the unexpected. Their truck camper, Bridget, is warmed up and ready to go. Welcome aboard! There's always room for one more.

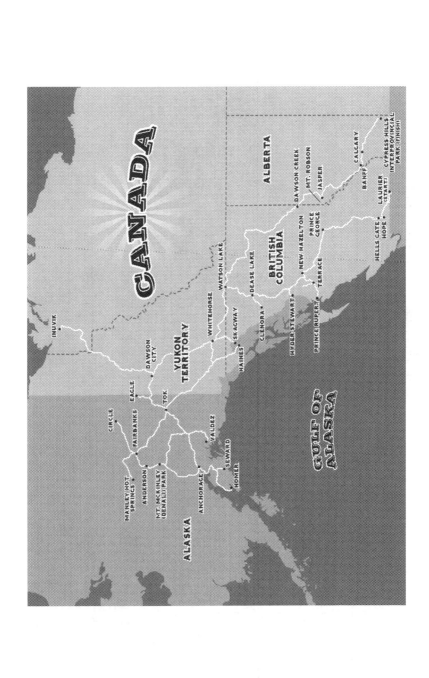

TABLE OF CONTENTS

1. Oh Canada 1
2. Hell's Gate. 6
3. Hatching a Good Fish Story 11
4. Unexpected Pleasure 18
5. Exquisite Exchamsiks 23
6. Sunless Prince Rupert 28
7. A 1995 Skeena. 32
8. Ride 'Em Cowboy! 38
9. Name This Town. 46
10. Our Secret. 52
11. Escape From Petersburg. 60
12. Canada's Daniel Boone 65
13. Into Each Life... 70
14. A Rainy Day in Whitehorse. 75
15. Do You Hear It? 81
16. A Haines Way of Life 87
17. The Pistol Packin' Parson. 92
18. A Treasured Tradition 99
19. The All Too Familiar. 104
20. Skagway and Dyea—The Tale of Two Towns 109
21. A Sense of Adventure 114
22. Arctic Greetings 121
23. Elvis Lives!. 129
24. The End of the Line. 135
25. A Hidden Gem 140
26. Double Oops! 146

27. Cap'n Hook 153
28. Things Are Looking Up 157
29. Forty Miles of Bad Road Plus 164
30. Strung Out in Anderson 169
31. Little Things Mean a Lot 174
32. Eight Cars in 160 Miles 179
33. There's Gold in Dem Thar Hills... 188
34. Been There, Done That! 193
35. Bears, Moose, Whales and Other Critters 197
36. Take a Hike! 206
37. I'm Bushed! 211
38. Cypress Hills Blues 217
Epilogue 221

1

OH CANADA

AFTER MUCH anticipation, we're finally in the land of the loonies and twonies, having crossed into our neighbor to the north at the border town of Cascade, British Columbia. Upon reflection, however, it hardly seems accurate to elevate Cascade to the status of town. In point of fact, together with its American equivalent, Laurier, the two barely constitute a wide spot in the road.

Before moving on, I should take the time to explain the reference to loonies and twonies. A loonie refers to the Canadian one dollar coin, so named because one side contains a large depiction of Canada's national bird, the loon.

I say this fully realizing the well-justified fervor among many Canadians for their beloved Canada Goose. I can just imagine if the goose had won out over the loon. Would we now be calling the Canadian one dollar coin the goosie? The mind boggles...

Anyway, when the government in Ottawa decided to introduce the two dollar coin, it just seemed natural somehow for this new currency to be nicknamed the twonie. Hence the reference to the land of the loonies and twonies!

In hindsight, it could be argued that, in the end, everything worked out for the best. Now we have loonies and twonies, rather than goosies and twosies!

I wonder why we Maughans get so excited when it comes to the process of crossing borders, especially for such an outwardly unremarkable experience. For my part, as the border approaches, the adrenaline begins a flowin' just that wee bit more and all senses seem more acute, as if in anticipation of a new and potentially memorable occurrence. Rarely, if ever, does the hype come near to matching the eventual reality. But this sense of excitement persists nonetheless.

Balancing out these mental gymnastics is the fact that the scenery on both sides of the border is basically the same, at least for the first 100 miles or so. And you'd be hard pressed to come up with any major differences in the way Americans and Canadians use the English language, at least in this part of Canada. But it must be allowed that they do have a "strange" way of pronouncing certain words. Just have a Canadian say "out and about" for instance, and your ears immediately will pick up on what I mean.

The Canadian customs official we had the good fortune to encounter duly noted our Texas license plates and despite our carefully cultivated, friendly demeanors proceeded to assume that, innocuously disguised, I was Clyde and Suzanne was my gun totin' moll, Bonnie. He seemed incredulous when told that no, we did not have any sort of weapon with us; that no, we did not own a weapon; and that no, we had never even fired a firearm in anger, or in self defense, for that matter. I could almost see him thinking: "But don't all Texans carry a gun of some sort, in addition to wearing those Stetson hats and pointy-toed cowboy boots?"

Not satisfied with those answers, he politely asked us to open up Bridget, our truck camper, and soon was going through her with the proverbial fine-tooth comb. In extremely firm and somber tones, he first read us our rights concerning potential prison time and vehicle confiscation if any gun, mace, pepper spray, tire iron or any other means of defense against the baddies were found in our possession.

I remember thinking at the time that I was indeed wise to have turned down what sounded like excellent advice to carry a baseball bat beside the driver's seat in the truck, just in case. But almost immediately my memory froze in horror as I remembered the three golf irons still lying in that exact spot. Oh my goodness, I could almost see the newspaper headlines: "Golf Clubs Cost Texas Couple Twenty Years In Jail!"

But, as it turned out, we were not meant to be jailbirds quite yet. After what seemed like an interminable time standing outside in the pouring rain, the unsuccessful search for contraband weapons, booze, cigarettes, etc., ended. We exchanged forced pleasantries and were finally on our way.

Talk about an obsession with weapons—he didn't even ask to see our passports, other forms of identification or insurance documents—nothing, zero, nada! We could have been international fugitives or, worse still, terrorists, for all he seemed to care. How about a little balance. And this was still several months before 9/11!

We were left to wonder, yet again, what it is about our particular rig, and truck campers in general, that seems to attract such intense scrutiny by Canadian border officials. Having Texas license plates is a definite impediment to smooth and easy border crossings into Canada. We fully understand, while disagreeing strongly with the false stereotyping. It should be noted that stereotyping all Canadians as hockey-playing Canucks would be just as inaccurate and ignorant.

Was it the way we acted with the officials that triggered something learned during their many courses in psychological profiling? Here, as with every other aspect of RVing, the advice on border crossing decorum by fellow travelers was both free, varied and not necessarily based on facts. "Don't act too happy or friendly" is one school of thought, counseling a very businesslike tone and a measured, not unfriendly, manner when dealing with such officials.

The other school of thought favors the ultra friendly, ultra organized approach, based on the premise that openness and transparency is the best modus operandi.

I wish I had the answer. I can tell you that we've tried it both ways with the same result—a search of our truck and camper, ranging from the perfunctory to quite thorough. So go figure. It could come down to a simple numbers game—search every third, sixth or eighth recreational vehicle, for instance, with the Maughans coming up snake eyes every time!

Another school of thought is that truck campers have gained an unsavory reputation with custom officers in general and Canadian officials in particular. Proponents of this theory say border officials think truck campers are the conveyance of choice for drug dealers, drug smugglers and other assorted criminal elements. The main reasons for this suspicion are twofold—the relative ease and speed of taking the camper and its contents off the truck and the truck camper's relatively low cost compared with its high-end cousins, the motor homes and fifth wheels.

Given all the complexities, there are those openly talking about the need to further streamline the processing of the massive amount and variety of traffic crossing the US-Canadian border. In fact, one recommendation by an ongoing joint task force between the two neighbors called for one building housing both custom and immigration officials from both countries.

Talk about the devil being in the details. I'm told that while adoption of the ideal led to the construction of some such buildings, relations rapidly deteriorated. Why, you might ask? Everything fell apart at one post when the Canadians strongly objected to and then banned their American counterparts from carrying their firearms when going to the bathrooms, which just happened to be located on the Canadian side of the building! Most likely, they had a bold, bright red, boundary line drawn right across the floors, ceilings, walls and any furniture that had the misfortune of getting in the way. I wonder what Martha Stewart would have thought about that decorating touch? So I guess it was a case of "back to the drawing board," as I haven't heard of any further progress in this regard.

And if this general tightening of security includes continued close scrutiny of Bridget, so be it. It's a price worth paying. Besides, when all is said and done, any notoriety, no matter how small, is better than none at all. And you know what, I do bear an uncanny resemblance to Clyde—pre-shootout, that is—if you discount that I'm old and grey and Mr. Barrow died in his early thirties!

2

HELL'S GATE

HYPERBOLE, OR hype, for short, is alive and well. What's more, it's not only living, but thriving, in Canada. In all fairness, that observation can be made about every other tourist spot in the world. Everything is touted as being the biggest, the fastest, the longest... you get the drift.

Not that I blame them for trying to part touristos from their dollars, yen, kwacha, euros, pounds, etc. After all, that's the name of the game—separation of cash from wallet or purse by any means, fair or foul. And they have the mounds of paraphernalia and other memorabilia on hand to help them reach that goal.

The only saving grace is that this stretching of the truth can, at times, become downright comical, bordering on the farcical. It's like those times we went to the circus as youngsters with the expectation of being awed and spellbound by the world's "strongest" man, complete with his requisite barbells. Another favorite might well have been the bearded lady with the hairiest face on any living female. Talk about the stuff of dreams or, occasionally, nightmares!

But just when your jaded, "been there, done that" mindset is about to get the better of you, salvation appears in the form of magnificent scenery so wide and grand it literally defies description. And what makes it all the more spectacular is the fact that it's ours for free, at least for now, until someone figures out a way of making us pay for its pleasures.

Take the Fraser Canyon for instance. It begins innocuously enough with little or no advanced notice of the scenic treasures that lie ahead. But before you know it you are surrounded by mountains which, depending on the time of year, are capable of receiving a dusting of snow right before your eyes.

Then slicing through them is the Fraser River, still providing a home for millions of spawning salmon, despite man's attempts to screw it up by damming the river in the 1920s.

One of the most spectacular stretches of the mighty Fraser occurs at a place appropriately called Hell's Gate. Here the might of the river is forced to squeeze through an ever-tightening noose of rock and overhanging ledge. But not of its own choosing.

All was well until 1914. It was in that year that the construction of a railroad line through Hell's Gate resulted in a huge rock slide, throttling the riverbed and almost ending in disaster for the millions of Sockeye salmon that call the Fraser and its many tributaries home. In fact, by 1921 the recorded catches of sockeye in the Fraser had dropped by more than one-third to just over 2,000,000.

Clearly something had to be done and done fast. But fast apparently isn't in the vocabulary of any government. So it wasn't until 1944 that something called the International Fishways was created.

To simplify a monumental and highly technical and complicated feat of engineering, the speed of the thundering Fraser through this man-made choke point was slowed to the point where the sockeye were given a fighting chance to spawn upstream. And apparently that's all the assistance the salmon needed as their numbers immediately began rebounding and have done so to this very day.

We got an up-close look at Hell's Gate and the eight fishways courtesy of an aerial tram (similar to those in the Swiss and Austrian Alps) that traverses the swirling river. And all for the paltry sum of 10 dollars per person. What a deal!

Given my fear of heights, I was somewhat apprehensive about riding the glass-enclosed tram. Not only does it descend just over 500 feet across the raging Fraser, but the prospect of falling into the millions of gallons of water pouring through the gorge every minute adds another layer of fear for the faint hearted!

A walk for only the brave hearted across Hell's Gate Canyon on British Columbia's Fraser River.

I wonder how many of you share my fears in such circumstances? Logic dictates that nothing tragic will happen as this particular tramway has had no accidents in its many years of service. Then why do I persist in thinking that the end is nigh the moment I step aboard? Go figure!

But they make the tramway ride well worthwhile. On the other side, the operators show a highly informative film about the annual salmon run. The film shows how the joint project in 1944 by the Canadians and the Americans saved the day when, by popular consensus, earlier greed and/or stupidity had combined to undo nature's best laid plans for the Sockeye salmon.

If spawning sockeyes find it tough sledding up the Fraser, much the same experience confronted the early settlers and explorers as they battled their way through the Fraser Canyon region. But both needed help—the salmon with their fishways and the pioneers with an almost equal number of tunnels for the roads and railway tracks that were to make the area accessible.

Although Hell's Gate is located in the town of Boston Bar, the actual Fraser River Valley begins just outside the town of Hope. By playing host to the throngs heading up or down the valley, Hope has gained quite a reputation of being the "Hollywood of the North." And the city is quite proud of its role as the backdrop for such movies as "Rambo: First Blood," starring Sylvester Stallone and Brian Dennehy, and Sidney Poitier's "Shoot to Kill." In fact, at various points throughout Hope, visitors can join the "Rambo walking tour"—a stop-by-stop description of scenes quite familiar to devotees of the Rambo experience!

But it was another equally compelling attraction that brought us to Hope. As a transplanted Aussie, I can smell a good meat pie or sausage roll miles away. And sure enough, once again my nose, highly attuned since childhood to such delicacies, didn't let me down and led us to a Swiss bakery. A meat pie, a sausage roll and, later, a mini apple strudel—and I was ready for a nap! Talk about a lack of willpower. But, then again, willpower has never been much of a match-up against the formidable duo of meat pies and sausage rolls!

In visiting Hope, Hell's Gate, and, later on, the lovely towns of Yale and Lytton, we had experienced the Fraser Canyon—a relatively short but demanding stretch of driving in terms of miles but an area containing a lifetime of spectacular scenic memories. But, as importantly, this region was to treat us to the first of several memorable scenic experiences in British Columbia and Yukon.

So listen up while I give you some free advice: when you're heading north to Alaska, don't get so caught up in the destination that you forget to stop and smell the roses. I can guarantee if you don blinders and put the pedal to the metal, you'll miss an awful lot of beautiful scenery. What's that about the journey being as important as the destination? We can tell you from experience that it's the absolute truth.

3

HATCHING A GOOD FISH STORY

THEY SAY confession is good for the soul. Having said that, there's something I must get off my chest. In fact, I'll go as far as to say that it's been a deep, dark secret of mine for many years. Here goes: I have a weakness for fish hatcheries and fish farms. There, I've said it! What a relief!

In fact, every time we drive past the sign for one I confess that my pulse quickens, resulting in an undeniable, almost uncontrollable, urge to go check it out. Why, it's almost as bad as seeing a sign for Dairy Queen, or DQ, as the ice cream chain is known north of the border!

It goes beyond the fact that I love fish, even though I must admit that's at the heart of the attraction. But there are other reasons as well.

First off, I love having the entire run of the place, with we two invariably being the lone visitors. And, as travelers know only too well, having scarcely any space to yourself at tourist stops can become extremely commonplace, especially if you're among the countless thousands trekking through British Columbia and beyond, during the height of the summer season.

Don't get me wrong. It's not that we're antisocial. But day after day of being cheek and jowl with other folks, no matter how amiable, gets to be a little old. And I'm sure they share my sentiments and would rather not see my mug in front of them all the time either!

Secondly, the atmosphere at fish hatcheries or fish farms is most always very friendly. No, I'll take it a step further. I'd go as far as to say that the staff at such facilities welcomes visitors with open arms.

Let's face it, as interesting and important as they are, such places are not exactly on most tourists' must-see list. So just the fact that you've taken the time and have shown the interest makes you special in their eyes.

And that leads me to the second reason we love fish hatcheries and farms so much. The workers, be they government employees or from private industry, can't do enough to make your stay memorable. Not only do you get that one-on-one royal treatment almost unheard of nowadays on the tourist trail, but their love and enthusiasm for their work shines through as they shower you with more facts than you'll ever remember.

That was our experience, thanks to a very enthusiastic young man named Corey, who greeted us after we had made a short detour off Highway 16 just about eight miles west of the town of Smithers. Our destination was the Toboggan Creek Salmon Hatchery or, to be more precise, the Toboggan Creek Salmon and Steelhead Enhancement Society.

During the course of Corey's extensive and fascinating personal tour, we were happy to learn that, in 2001 at least, the salmon situation in his region, with the lamentable exception of the Coho, was very healthy, despite all the doom and gloom reported in the popular press.

Now having said that, I realize I have to be extremely careful when making such sweeping statements about salmon, a subject that's highly sensitive and emotional, especially throughout northwestern United States and Canada. The issue of overfishing lies at the core of these mutual hard feelings.

Corey was happy to announce that the total number of salmon finding their way home to spawn in Toboggan Creek, after navigating the Bulkley River and others, was up from 6,000 two years earlier to an estimated 14,000.

Corey also gave us a quick primer on the three types of salmon—Coho, Chinook and Steelhead—that call Toboggan Creek and its associated waterways home. As he rattled off their many differences, the biggest, to our uninformed minds, was this: whereas the Coho and Chinook only make it back one time to spawn, some Steelhead successfully run the gauntlet to spawn year after year. And to my mind, that really makes Steelheads salmon among salmon!

Our personal guide noted that while all the various species have their own peculiar challenges in the Bulkley River system, most of the current worry is centered on the Coho, which is described as being endangered, while the numbers of Steelhead and Chinook are designated as adequate.

At this point you might well be asking the same question I was pondering: what's the general route these salmon have to take to get home? Well, after entering the Yukon, they take a right turn at one of its many tributaries, the Skeena, then swim into the smaller Bulkley and from there into the Toboggan, which is just one of many streams and creeks that feed into the Bulkley. And all we're talking about here is a few thousand miles—one way!

In a nutshell, this is how the hatchery operates. As the returning salmon swim upstream to spawn in Toboggan Creek and nearby rivers and streams, hatchery staff catch a designated number of Coho and Chinook, removing eggs for incubation before releasing the fish to complete their journey. These eggs are then placed in plastic bags along with sperm, (in the case of salmon, the sperm is called milt) before everything is hustled back to the hatchery to begin the incubation process. Now comes the tricky part. The collected eggs and milt will only do their thing, so to speak, if the hatchery is able to fool ole Mother Nature into thinking they are in the wild. The Toboggan Creek Hatchery (and others, I'm sure) is able to re-create these natural conditions by allowing only gravity-fed water to flow through indoor racks of flat mesh boxes in the same way that stream water runs through the gravel nests of their wild counterparts.

This hatchery operates without the use of a single pump. As I said earlier, the secret to their success is the fact that the water has to be gravity fed, thus simulating the conditions found in the salmon's natural habitat.

The eggs hatch as little fish: now there's a news bulletin for you! Called alevins, they don't have to be fed, as they live off egg sacks hanging from their bellies. When they eat up the contents of those sacks they earn the right to be termed fry. And so they won't remain "small fry," they must be fed every 15 minutes each day for the next nine months. Along the way, the fry are also microscopically tagged to aid in the short and long-term research into just where they go and exactly what they do after being set free.

About a year after hatching, the salmon, much larger now but still comparatively quite tiny, are ready to be called smolts. Now they only need to be fed three or four times a day. But when they do chow down, hold on to your hat, because without a word of exaggeration, the water is suddenly transformed into a boiling pot of shimmering silver! No table manners here, folks. It's survival of the fittest... and fastest to that food.

As is the case with each step of the process, much care

is given to simulate wild conditions, and after 18 months the salmon are ready to be released.

No scooping them up by the bucket full and dumping them unceremoniously into the waterways. No sirree! These pampered piscine are afforded every dignity in rejoining their wild cousins or maybe even their long lost brothers and sisters.

It's done this way. There are screens that separate the outdoor pens or holding tanks from Toboggan Creek itself. These screens are simply removed, allowing the smolts the freedom to swim out and join their wild counterparts whenever their instinct dictates.

Despite all these efforts to make their stay at places like the Toboggan Creek Hatchery as natural and environmentally friendly as possible, the argument still rages as to whether or not these salmon have the potential of somehow damaging the "wild" salmon population not afforded these "luxuries" of early life. The arguments both pro and con are heated, passionate and quite persuasive and will continue without true resolution.

It was also interesting to learn that, despite media reports to the contrary, Corey and his fellow hatchery workers had no problems whatsoever with their American counterparts when it came to sharing vital salmon-related information. In fact, Corey said they had just recently received a call from Alaskan fishery officials telling them when they could expect the first Steelheads to arrive in Toboggan Creek.

Predictably, we asked the question that I'm willing to bet is asked by every visitor to such a facility—just how do these remarkable fish navigate the thousands of miles back to this exact tiny body of water? Although he's answered the very same question countless times, Corey patiently and expertly went through the various scientific theories behind this truly phenomenal feat of navigation, perseverance and endurance.

It's all to do with the sun, the stars and instincts. Trust me!

But somehow I have to believe each and every salmon has had its very own tiny built-in GPS tracking unit long before we came up with the technology. In fact, it wouldn't surprise me to find out that we actually learned the secrets from these navigational geniuses!

Talk about running the gauntlet. After spending several seasons somewhere off the coast of Alaska in the Bering Sea, the Steelhead and their cousins—the Chinook, the Coho, the Pink, the Chum, the Sockeye and Coastal Cutthroat—have to somehow evade thousands of trawler nets, the hooks and fish wheels of countless recreational, traditional and commercial fishermen along the Yukon and its tributaries, the claws and jaws of hungry bears, numerous artificial fishways and other potential obstacles just to make it home again.

Of course many don't make it and wind up either as dinner or above some mantelpiece somewhere along the way. But Corey said enough do (with the current exception being the Coho) reach their destination to give hope that this mighty symbol of the northwest will continue to play its rightful role as a dominant economic, recreational and gastronomical force in the lives of so many, if, of course, managed judiciously. But that's a mighty big if!

In all fairness, I must report that most all our attempts to get a good grilled salmon steak dinner ended in abject failure. I don't want to leave the impression that finding fresh salmon in local restaurants was impossible. Maybe we were just unlucky and were looking in the wrong places or, to be more precise, wrong eating establishments.

But I think it's something approaching weird. Here you have rivers at various times of the year nearly choking with all these varieties of salmon. But when we asked about seafood restaurants serving local salmon we invariably received a blank stare in return. I just don't get it.

But then there's always the don't-you-dare-miss exception that goes a long way towards knocking such theories to a cocked hat. And one of those exceptions is most certainly the Klondike Rib and Salmon Barbecue Restaurant in downtown Whitehorse, Yukon. In fact, I'd go as far as to say that the food there, especially the salmon, is worth driving a 100 miles out of your way.

Suffice it to say, any trip through British Columbia, Yukon and, of course, Alaska would be incomplete and approaching meaningless without some encounter with one species of salmon or another. So be it on a riverbank, from a boat on some larger body of water or, from our favorite vantage point, in a restaurant gazing down on a hunk of one grilled, smoked or barbecued, salmon is an integral part of the overall North-to-Alaska experience.

After all, how can you can truly say you "did" the Northwest without having a few salmon stories to brag about to friends and family back home. And maybe, just maybe, some of them might even be true!

4

UNEXPECTED PLEASURE

EVERY NOW and then, the rather blasé, even thoroughly jaded, traveler stumbles on the truly unexpected—something that because of its exquisite beauty etches itself on the memory forever. And in this day of travel one upsmanship, such a claim is rare indeed.

If you look for Vetter Falls on your typical tourist maps or in your average travel book, good luck. In fact, even local literature for the traveler seems to be a willing accomplice in keeping this gem a well-kept secret. Good for them, since they obviously know a wonderful thing when they see it!

But, you might argue, why is this big blabbermouth spilling the beans and, in the process, making the secret of Vetter Falls a secret no more? I plead guilty, with extenuating circumstances.

For all its incredible beauty, Vetter Falls is hardly on the tourist's beaten path. Situated about 30 miles north of the city of Terrace, British Columbia, in an area of dried lava flows (much more about that later), the falls have few signs indicating their existence. In fact, it was more by chance than by design that we took the time to walk the short distance from the road to see them. All this is by way of saying this particular gem must be sought out, thus discouraging the flood of humanity that invariably ruins the moment.

Picture a small, pristine, bubbling stream cascading not just over one modest fault line, but over two other smaller but equally beautiful drop-offs. Place all three of these lovely waterfalls in a small amphitheater of towering, lightly drooping, evergreens and your mind's eye is fast envisioning the almost mystical mood created.

Vetter Falls—the hidden gem of Nisga'a
Memorial Lava Bed Provincial Park.

If you're looking for the kind of majestic scenic experience that makes you gasp, Vetter Falls will fall short, way short. Rather, the falls offer a softer experience, a chance for introspection and indeed reflection amid sighs of appreciation for the feelings of peace and tranquility engendered. This is a place of renewal, a place at which to linger and a place where much film will be used in a vain attempt to capture the bucolic splendor.

Taking up positions on waterside boulders, we sat in almost reverential silence, with only the sounds of an occasional bird and the gurgling waters breaking our reverie. To be sure, our experience was enhanced immeasurably by having this almost magical place all to ourselves—hence the need for secrecy!

That's not the end of the story of this seeming wonderland. Adding to the charm is the fact that the stream quickly disappears beneath a bed of lava deposited two kilometers wide and up to 100 feet deep by a volcanic eruption about 250 years ago.

Not only did Canada's last known eruption kill 2,000 of the local Nisga'a First Nation peoples, but its action also trapped a population of Steelhead salmon. Entering their spawning grounds, the steelheads found their way had been blocked by this barrier of lava. And over the course of thousands of generations, these salmon have changed both their color and shape, coming to look more like snakes in appearance as they adapted to their predicament.

I don't know about you but I love such stories. As tragic as their original circumstances, the Steelhead salmon found a way not only to survive but to thrive—yet another story of adaptation and Mother Nature's ingenuity in her constant search for infinite variety.

As lovely as they are, the Vetter Falls are just one of many interesting features of the Nisga'a Memorial Lava Bed Provincial Park. And one of the best parts of it all was the fact that we only had to share the park with two other people—a German couple in a rental camper. We played tag with them as we visited the various volcanic sites, to the point where it became something of a game. Fun and games between two sets of vagabonds out on the almost barren, moon-like terrain still held hostage to its violent past!

Likewise, we also had the park campground almost to ourselves, sharing it with a garrulous older Dutch couple, Nick and Wilhelmina, in the midst of a seven-week tour of western Canada in a rental van. It was great fun sharing a laugh or two with them and once again realizing that travelers share that unique common bond.

We exchanged travel tips and stories about our families. No full names were asked for or given as both sides rather sadly accepted that, while quite pleasurable, this represented a chance, fleeting encounter, to be repeated only in our memories.

When not talking to our new Dutch friends, we were busy admiring what can only described as living behemoths—gigantic, moss-covered trees so mammoth but so vulnerable to man's avarice for a quick buck. I can't imagine anyone having the heart to put saw or ax to these magnificent works of nature—works hundreds of years in the making.

Walking among them is not to embrace all the radical environmentalist doctrines. It's simply to put the question: "What if successive generations were denied this experience? Surely they would be the poorer for it." But for the foreseeable future these trees are safe.

Even though the Nisga'a Memorial Lava Bed Park is a part of British Columbia's provincial system, it's administered on a daily basis by the Nisga'a First Nation peoples.

They're still getting up to speed in the complicated system of presenting the diverse features of this park. And the sign posting and illustrations leave something to be desired.

But, on the other hand, it was most pleasant not to have to contend with the slick commercialism so prevalent at similar parks elsewhere. So while we had to hunt a little harder to find a certain point of interest and then have our imagination tested upon arrival, we came to appreciate and respect the Nisga'a for encouraging visitors to respect this place—the burial ground for more than 2,000 of their ancestors.

5

EXQUISITE EXCHAMSIKS

"EXCHAMSIKS RIVER Provincial Park. Located fifty-six kilometers west of Terrace on Highway Sixteen. Near confluence of Exchamsiks and Skeena Rivers, set in old-growth forest of giant Sitka spruce. Dry toilets, boat launch, salmon fishing, cash only, pets on leash. Open May to Sept."

Not exactly scintillating stuff. But, then again, and in all fairness, that rather bare bones, matter of fact description did come from a tourist giveaway magazine listing British Columbia's top 350 campgrounds. In other words, Exchamsiks River Provincial Park was competing with 349 other provincial campgrounds for special attention.

I realize that brevity is the soul of wit, but c'mon, be honest, if you didn't have any prior knowledge, is that the type of descriptive information that would have you making a beeline to spend camping time at Exchamsiks over all others? I doubt it.

Mind you, this doesn't constitute any type of criticism because, as far as it goes, that cryptic description of Exchamsiks River Provincial Park is entirely accurate. My point is that it, in no way, shape or form, prepares one for the absolute picture postcard beauty awaiting there.

As the saying goes, sometimes it's better to be lucky than

good. Having had our finances somewhat battered and bruised from a series of major repairs to our truck and camper in Terrace, we were just looking for a place to park Bridget for the night and lick our fiscal wounds before heading off down this portion of the Yellowhead Highway to the city of Prince Rupert on the coast.

We fully intended to stay just the one evening. We ended up staying three glorious days and then, only reluctantly, moved on due to the pressures of time. To be fair, I must admit our stay was made extra special by camping's luck of the draw. But more about that in just a minute.

Entering the park off of Highway 16, you're immediately taken through a forest of trees described in best understated terms as lofty. In point of fact, what we were experiencing were literally acres of one of the last major stands of mighty Sitka spruce towering skywards for hundreds of feet. Suzanne put it best when she said it was like being in a hardwood cathedral, thousands of years in the making. Amen to that!

I'm told, as hard as it is to imagine, that not so long ago such forests of Sitka spruce were commonplace—that is, until the logging industry came to British Columbia and the sound of "timber!" rang out millions of times throughout the province. Now that the mighty Sitka has been brought to the very edge of extinction – at least in British Columbia – it is revered and carefully protected. And walking through them I can certainly see why.

Words like "majestic," "regal" and "awe-inspiring" come to mind. But singularly, or in combination, they don't come close to doing justice to these relics of a bygone era. As travelers are wont to say, you have to see them to appreciate them!

But while this experience was truly magnificent, the best was still to come. Unbeknownst to us at the time, the road was winding down to the far end of the park and the three remaining campsites in a clearing on the banks of the Exchamsiks River itself.

Folks, I've done my share of camping and sightseeing, but the scene that unfolded in front of us was worthy of being on one of those postcards sent to friends and family back home. And to make the situation even better, only two of three campsites were occupied. That's what I mean about it being better to be lucky than good!

I think the ultimate compliment to the magnificence of the view before us was the fact that I could hardly wait to bring Bridget to a stop before reaching for the camera. Now I'm known to be an inveterate picture taker but not to this degree of fervor and urgency.

The camping spot with a million dollar view at the Exchamsiks River
Provincial Park on the road to Prince Rupert, British Columbia.

It was as if I were afraid that all this scenic perfection would suddenly evaporate before I had the chance to capture it on film. But when viewing the end result of my photographic frenzy I still feel the frustration of not having been able to fully capture the sublime beauty before us.

As we all know, photos are one-dimensional, and cameras are unable to capture the mood and the total serenity engendered by the locale being photographed. And that was where the photos fell short. It was as if we had been dropped into this magical, visually perfect, realm that left us both spellbound. And all we had was a mere camera to try to capture it.

Before us were the blue-green waters of the Exchamsiks—water that reflected the surrounding snow-capped peaks and the towering Sitka spruces. Adding to the splendor were three days of clear sunny weather which lent extra sparkle and definition to our awesome surroundings.

For the fisherman (which I am not) the Exchamsiks is renowned for being literally choked with Cutthroat trout and various types of salmon. In fact, the park ranger told me that there's no limit on the daily catch of cutthroat, with a license of course.

But not everyone or everything needs such permission. Although we never got a true fix on their species, what appeared to be otters busied themselves with their daily catching and dining on the river's piscine bounty as well. Clearly there were enough fish to go around.

Maybe they were seals or sea lions, as our campsite was right near the confluence of the Exchamsiks with the much bigger and treacherous Skeena, world-renowned for the size and quality of the salmon caught there. I say treacherous because the river has been known to rise up to 17 feet in a single day.

In addition, it's generally conceded that the mighty Skeena is one of North America's toughest, if not the very toughest, rivers to navigate. And that's exactly what steamboats did but very methodically and with a great deal of skill and care. In fact, the hour-and-a-half drive between Terrace and Prince Rupert used to take sternwheelers an average of 35 hours.

But that was many years ago. In fact, the last sternwheeler, the Inlander, made her final journey in September, 1912, ending only 22 years of riverboat activity on the Skeena. The vagaries of navigating the Skeena and, more importantly, the arrival of the railroad helped hasten the end of that particular industry.

So as you're belting down the Yellowhead Highway towards Prince Rupert and you hit the 34-mile mark out of Terrace, if you need a little therapeutic R&R (and who doesn't now and then), just follow the signs to Exchamsiks River Provincial Park. The majestic Sitka spruces will be there waiting to welcome you and if you're lucky, truly lucky, so will one of those three idyllic riverside camping spots at the very end of the park. Then and only then will you truly be fully able to understand what I've been raving about. Enjoy!

6

SUNLESS PRINCE RUPERT

"Please tell me what the sun looks like." When you think about it, that's not the kind of request most travelers look forward to asking, especially when they're hoping to do their summer sightseeing accompanied by blue skies and bright sunshine.

But that, indeed, was our lament after enduring several days of almost ceaseless rain in the city of Prince Rupert, located on the British Columbia coast just a hop, skip and a jump south of the Alaskan Panhandle. Almost despairing of the very existence of that life-giving star, the sun, my desperation led me to seek out the manager of the now quite soggy and boggy campground at which we were staying.

Upon reflection, I really don't quite know what I was hoping for. Was I looking for solace, a shoulder to cry on? Well, if so, I'd certainly looked in the wrong direction. As it turned out, the manager hailed from Scotland so all I got was an "Aaah laddie. Isn't the weather grand? Around here we call this lovely soft persistent rain liquid sunshine."

Sure, sure. Thanks for nothing. A lot of good that did my sagging psyche. I might as well have saved my breath!

To be as fair as possible, Prince Rupert's prevailing weather conditions should hardly have caught us by surprise. In fact, every tour guide, even the usual glowing local variety, forthrightly addresses the phenomenon of the incessant rains. So no visitor, no matter how disappointed, can accuse the various writers of being part of some monstrous cabal, somehow conspiring against telling the truth, the whole truth and nothing but the truth.

But my cynical mind tells me that Prince Rupert's local tourist board really doesn't have any option other than to 'fess up. I mean they can hardly advertise Prince Rupert as rivaling Miami or some other sun-splashed mecca when quite the opposite is true. And even though quite fanciful in concept, they realize all too well that the liquid sunshine gambit would wear thin in a New York minute.

So in what can only be described as a surprisingly frank and honest observation on Prince Rupert's weather, it's observed that this city of around 18,000 inhabitants gets, on average, no less than 93 inches of this "liquid sunshine" every year. Or to put it another way, it's marginally more than one inch of rain every four days. Wow—keep the umbrellas and slickers at the ready—that is, if you can ever get them dry!

Not withstanding the average of 93 inches of moisture per year, Prince Rupert came within an eyelash of becoming Canada's largest west coast city. That's right, the largest, Vancouver notwithstanding.

The story goes like this. Charles Hays, one of Canada's leading industrialists at the turn of the century, fell in love with the city of Prince Rupert. Yes, he loved the scenery, the fishing and the people. But what he loved most of all was the fact that the town overlooked Canada's deepest and northernmost ice-free harbors. And, as a businessman, Mr. Hays had visions of making Prince Rupert the main western terminus of a second transcontinental railway across Canada.

Seemingly, Prince Rupert's future glory was assured. But then cruel fate stepped in. On his way back from Europe to set this grand scheme in motion, Mr. Hays made a fatal decision that was to change Prince Rupert's fortunes forever. He chose to return to Canada on a vessel named the HMS Titanic. And that was the name of that tune, as Baretta of American television fame once put it. And since Charles Hays was the driving force behind the Prince Rupert venture, his plans for the town's grand future died with him.

I rather like Prince Rupert just the way it turned out—a smallish but rather cosmopolitan city in its own unique, soggy way. Pottering around the town's lovely downtown area, we were impressed with its well-appointed museums, especially the Museum of Northern British Columbia, and its varied and excellent restaurants.

As one would imagine, the city's seafood restaurants drew the lion's share of patrons. But a real find for those with a more eclectic palate was Herby's—a restaurant specializing in, of all things, Vietnamese and Canadian cuisines.

Why Vietnamese on the menu? Well, in the early twentieth century, the seafood industry enticed many Vietnamese immigrants to Prince Rupert hoping the economy would benefit from their considerable expertise. They came, they succeeded and they stayed, lending their distinct cultural flavor to this most interesting of cities.

That having been said, one has to want to visit Prince Rupert, as it's hardly on the beaten path taken by most folks heading hastily north to Alaska with blinkers on. The drive to Prince Rupert from the small aluminum smelting community of Kitimat took us not only through the crossroads town of Terrace but also from bright sunshine to an increasing number of clouds lying low along the snowcapped mountains that wedged us in against the shallow but lovely Skeena River. Could rain be far behind?

We drove along Highway 16 with an increasing awareness that the ocean was just before us, filling the air with a faint salty aroma and proving a magnetic attraction for the Skeena as its churning waters accelerated their headlong dash to the sea.

Somehow the sea holds a singular attraction for me. So come what may, we generally find ourselves taking a long walk along the seashore, every now and then perching on rocks just to watch the waves and smell the seaweed. Prince Rupert also afforded us that opportunity.

It was during one of those walks that I struck up the acquaintance of a local gardener out taking advantage of a lovely sunny day. While sharing a glorious view of the deep-water harbor so coveted by industrialist Mr. Hays, my new friend thoroughly agreed with my assessment that, in the end, all had worked out for the best. And, she said, our assessment of Prince Rupert's past chance at industrial glory was undoubtedly shared by the many whales that come into view from her kitchen window.

7

A 1995 SKEENA

WHAT BOUQUET... what a delight to the palate... and what a year! Non, pardon monsieur, I'm not talking about a bottle of the very finest vintage wine from France, California, or perhaps even Australia's famed Barossa Valley. Rather, this is a reference to an expertly prepared mason jar of aged salmon.

The 1995 Skeena will forever be linked to Rob Snider, who in a twinkling of an eye, managed to transform himself from total stranger to dear, dear friend. And, just like a fine vintage, this salmon from the Skeena River had also been aged to perfection, thanks in great measure to Rob's masterful fishing and canning skills.

Rob Snider is one of those rare individuals who almost willed folks to like him right off the bat. But unbeknownst to him, that natural-born ability was to be put to the sternest of tests by a couple of self-styled Grumpy Gus's.

You see, Suzanne and I had pulled into this particular campground on the outskirts of the town of Terrace in quite a foul mood. Yes, indeed, we thought we had every right to engage in one big pity party, given the perilous state of our pride and joy, a 2000 Ford F-350 diesel dually super cab truck.

Bridget, named after St. Bridget, the Celtic saint of travelers, was the culprit. The truck camper was literally ripping apart our truck, beginning where it's attached to both sides of the truck right behind its super cab doors. It takes lots of raw energy to rip a three-inch gash in reinforced steel plating. But that's exactly what had happened and now something had to be done, and done fast, to fix that potentially dangerous situation.

When the folks at the RV dealership mounted it that way, I guess they never figured on the extra stresses and strains that would be exerted on the entire unit during the long and often difficult journey north through British Columbia, Yukon, Northwest Territories and Alaska. And being novices at living in our truck camper all the time we had neither the expertise nor the courage to question the efficacy of such a deployment. It was a case of "they must know what they're doing"—a most dangerous assumption, as subsequent experience taught us.

So here we were in Terrace, hoping against hope that this small RV repair shop could install these so-called "belly bars" we'd been hearing so many good things about since arriving north of the border.

Mounted front and rear, the bars are welded right to the truck frame as a way of providing extra stability. Not only do they help eliminate the rock and roll sway, the accompanying longer tie-downs also help reduce unnecessary camper movement. This was the lesson we were about to learn, albeit the hard, costly way, about the wisdom and safety of having our camper attached to the truck down low rather than up high.

As we sat there bemoaning our fate and waiting for the RV repair shop to open, we noticed we had inherited a very curious visitor. For right now he seemed content to circle our rig peering very intently at it from every conceivable angle.

Still determined to be somewhat antisocial, we figured if we just paid him no mind he'd eventually get the hint and go on his way. But, as I related earlier, we hadn't counted on Rob's winning... and persistent... ways. So it wasn't all that much later that Rob found himself being invited into our rig for the so-called "Cook's tour."

Isn't it amazing how easily new friends can be made when we're not even trying? I mean, one rarely wakes up in the morning saying: "Let's go out and make a new friend today!" Somehow it just doesn't seem to work that way, at least not for us. But, sometimes, under the most unlikely circumstances, things just click. Then, before you know it, a new friendship is born.

Such was the case with this personable young man, who couldn't have been more than 25 years old. Despite his relative youth, Rob was a walking, talking tourist department. If he didn't know about it, it wasn't worth knowing! In fact, I doubt whether there was anything noteworthy going on within a 100 mile radius that Rob didn't know about.

For instance, he asked if we knew about that weekend's Kispiox Valley Rodeo. Yeah, right. Here our truck is practically falling apart before our very eyes and we're supposed to be thinking about going to a rodeo!

Surely we'd visited Mt. Rocher Deboule that towers over his hometown of Hazelton? Again, vacant stares.

What about fishing and hunting? Did we do any? Had we eaten local salmon or moose? Man oh man, did this youngster ever have the gift of the gab! All I could think of was my late mom in Australia. One of her favorite sayings concerned someone's ability to talk the bottom off an iron pot! Come to think of it, I wouldn't have bet against Rob being able to do just that!

But you know what? The more Rob peppered us with these and seemingly thousands of other questions, the more his obvious enthusiasm proved infectious. Before we knew it, we found ourselves looking beyond belly bars and rips in the side of trucks. One way or the other, we realized, these annoyances would pass and that it was now time again to go adventure hunting, or, as we like to call it, "memory making."

Then, inevitably, it was time for Rob to leave. "See you later" or "Stay in touch" hardly seemed appropriate or adequate, given the circumstances and intensity of our meeting.

Once again Rob came to our rescue. He asked us to meet him at such-and-such a time, in such-and-such a place, in Hazelton, where he'd show us around and introduce us to some of the local folks and scenery, including, I might add, Mt. Rocher Deboule.

It's one of those times when you take up the invitation, not truly knowing if it's for real or just another way of ending a conversation. But, in the end, we thought, "What the heck. We have nothing to lose and he does seem like such a nice, genuine young man!"

Reflecting back on Rob's parting remarks, we seemed to recall that he said something about giving us a jar or two of local salmon he had caught and preserved. But, then again, many good folks promise lots of things, with little or no intention of ever making good. So it's a case of in one ear and out the other!

Well, at the appointed time and place we sat parked awaiting the arrival of our newfound friend. The rendezvous hour came and went and no Rob.

Expecting the worst but hoping for the best, I went to check up on him, only to be told that he had left to pick up a few things. But we were told quite emphatically that he had left strict instructions that we were to stay put for as long as it took for him to return.

Fair enough, at least he'd done us that courtesy. Well, about half an hour later, who should appear—loaded down with a black plastic sack filled to the top? You guessed it—Rob.

Now he really had our curiosity whetted. What the heck was in that plastic sack? To our sheer gastronomical delight, it was, in fact, loaded to the gunwales with the widest assortment of frozen and preserved fish and game we'd ever seen.

Let's start with the frozen moose. There were moose steaks, minced moose, haunches of moose, moose burgers—you name it and there it lay, just waiting to be thawed and enjoyed.

You say you like salmon. Not only were there mounds of frozen fillets, there were countless jars of preserved salmon, each one in its own mason jar and carefully documented as to where and when the fish was caught. Hence, the name: "A '95 Skeena."

But where to store this unexpected cornucopia of goodies? The preserved salmon was a no-brainer. We'd just put most of the jars in our tiny basement compartment, being careful to individually wrap each one to avoid breakage. Just thinking of the fish stench that would surely follow any such breakage would insure that the job was done with the greatest of care.

And what to do with what must have been more than 25 pounds of assorted packages of frozen moose? For folks with larger rigs and correspondingly larger refrigerators and freezers, no worries, right? Not so with our tiny freezer. But somehow, and, to this very day, I really don't know how, Suzanne managed to shoehorn all of that moose and salmon into that tiny space. She has a special talent for that sort of thing!

How do you thank a person for such a wonderful display of friendship and generosity? Somehow a mere thank you doesn't quite cut it. But Rob, to his ever-lasting credit, wanted nothing more, even though I did manage to get him to accept an Alaskan tee shirt, which I sent him months later.

Talk about the gift that keeps on giving! It took us several months to work our way through that bountiful largesse.

And every time we sank our teeth into some of that moose or salmon, we thought of Rob Snider and the amazing serendipities of this wonderful lifestyle.

So here's to you, Rob, and thanks for the terrific memories. And here's also to the long-empty mason jar that once held that scrumptious vintage salmon with the truly memorable name: "A 1995 Skeena!"

8

RIDE 'EM COWBOY!

HAVE YOU ever been to a rodeo? C'mon, you can stop snickering now. Remember what they say about the only silly question being the one you're afraid to ask!

You have to understand that Suzanne and I are just a couple of tenderfeet (or is that tenderfoots?) with a gaping hole in our life resumes. So you can imagine how excited we were to literally stumble upon the chance to fill that cultural void in arguably one of the more unlikely of spots, the small town of Kispiox, British Columbia.

But I'm here to tell you that although small in size when compared with the biggies such as the Calgary Stampede or the Cheyenne Frontier Days, the Kispiox Valley Rodeo had it all. And when I say all, I mean all—saddle bronc riding, bareback riding, team roping, calf roping, ladies' barrel racing, plus my favorite, steer wrestling. And this is not counting all the important junior competitions, which proved to be not only a real hoot but show stoppers as well!

So you could say the Kispiox Rodeo had something for everyone. But would or could you expect less from an event billing itself humbly as the biggest little rodeo in the west!

Mind you, it's not like the organizers' collective ego had run amok. They were, in fact, referring to western British Columbia and not the geographical entity south of the border.

While that may well be splitting hairs, ultimately it's the tale of the turnstiles that matters. So if the marketing hype was designed to put the maximum number of bums in seats it was certainly a huge success.

To my admittedly untrained eye, this particular event was more, much more, than your garden-variety rodeo. Since its founding in 1952, the Kispiox Valley Rodeo has managed to re-invent itself as something approaching an excellent venue for the good folks of the surrounding countryside to celebrate their decidedly hardy, independent lives.

And to think we could have just as easily bypassed Kispiox and its rodeo on our travels north along the Stewart-Cassier Highway. In fact, the Kispiox Valley Rodeo wasn't even on our collective radar screens when fate intervened in the form of Rob Snider.

As noted earlier, we had met Rob in Terrace while making RV repairs and a friendship quickly followed. At that time, Rob asked if we were planning to attend a local rodeo that was being held that coming Sunday. Describing it as better than proverbial sliced bread (well almost), he sold us in no time. After all, it wasn't as if we had a tight schedule to follow! And Alaska and other destinations north could most certainly wait for the mighty Maughans a couple more days.

Officially, the Kispiox Valley Rodeo is a one-day affair. That particular year it was held on a Sunday. But I'm not sure that's always the case. That's only relevant in noting that true to the rodeo's extra social component the locals came early, like Friday, and stayed late, many leaving sometime Monday, and then only reluctantly.

We arrived around noon on Friday amid frenetic prepara-tions, mostly concerning the thousand and one rodeo-related chores needing attention. Competing for immediate attention were the untold number of ancillary "emergencies" such as vehicle parking, the slotting of folks into rough and ready camping sites, the assigning of booths and general space for the many vendors and so on.

Good humor was the order of the day, with an extra dollop thrown in for good measure when our Texas license plates were spotted upon our arrival. Amid much good-natured ribbing and banter, we were asked to please check our six shooters at the main office. We were also requested not to block the view of others by wearing our 40-litre hats (10 gallon to us non metrics) during the competition!

Agreeing to comply fully and promising to curb our natural Texas rowdiness, we were quickly off to find a boondocking site, most of which already had been snapped up by the come-early-and-stay-late crowd. But they had missed a premium spot fairly close to the main venue so the veteran Texans snatched it up very smartly!

As noted earlier, while the main attraction was Sunday's rodeo, the folks had come to satisfy other needs as well. Impromptu jam sessions had already sprung up hither and yon, horses and other stock were tethered here and there, and friendships, old and brand new, were in full bloom throughout.

In fact, you only needed to step outside of truck or camper to be set upon and engaged in friendly banter. Once again, our Texas plates proved a genuine icebreaker.

We quickly found that a certain curiosity surrounded folks driving into a small rodeo grounds north of the border in a rig sporting Lone Star State license plates. I got the distinct impression that many thought I was most likely a former bareback rider, calf roper or, God forbid, a Brahma bull rider! I know I look a little rough around the edges but that's really rubbing salt in the wound!

By the way, while we're on this subject, I'd like to know why I'm always assumed to be a "former"? It must have something to do with my grey hair—that is, where I even have hair!

I must say this quasi-celebrity status was most likely enhanced by the quality and general appearance of our truck and camper when compared with many of the other rigs on site. But, to be fair, these others were working rigs so they had earned their worth many times over.

While the temptation was certainly there to falsify my non-existent rodeo credentials, I always managed to step back from the precipice. Maybe it was that tiny, yet persistent warning voice cautioning that chutzpah can only get you so far, especially given the reality that I barely know one end of a horse or bull from the other!

Because of our Texas plates, we were also asked whether we knew or were friends of the very popular Neil Gibson of Arlington, Texas. Once again, Neil was sponsoring the featured event, the Marty Allen Memorial Saddle Bronc Riding competition. Neil puts up the 2,000 dollar purse and the hand-tooled gold and silver buckle that goes with the top prize money.

Unfortunately, we've never met Mr. Gibson, but when things finally got under way we too became rodeo experts. With our 40-liter hats carefully put to one side, we cheered when others cheered, we groaned on cue and, paying close attention, we soon had the vital rodeo lingo down pat.

For instance, Brahma bulls are not mean and evil. They are bad-tempered—a necessary attitude for any self-respecting Brahma hoping to be invited to such an affair. It's as if there's a rule posted at every rodeo grounds entrance: "No sweet tempered or docile Brahmas need apply!"

All too soon, it was time for the rodeo's grand finale, the Brahma bull riding. So with the calf roping, team roping, bareback riding, saddle bronc riding, ladies barrel racing all contested, it was now time for ole Twilight Zone, Hot Sauce, Play Station and Mr. Blue and their mates to do their thing. And did they ever!

I can see it now. It's about a half hour before they have the spotlight and ole Hot Sauce has all his fellow Brahmas huddled around him in their pen. In a speech that would have made Knute Rockne of Notre Dame fame proud, Hot Sauce gives them a pep talk. He exhorts them to not only send the local yokels flying as quickly as possible, but also to give them a little extra present as well!

And by golly, not a single bull lets down the team, all living up to their rank reputation. In fact, not one rider even comes close to staying aboard for the allotted eight seconds!

In all fairness, it must be said that the packed house had as much fun watching events on the other end of the danger scale. I'm talking about the special competitions for the young 'uns, such as the Stickhorse Race and the Mutton Derby.

Sheep running around with young children trying to hang on to their fleece is a guaranteed crowd favorite. And when you combine this with races involving upside down broom sticks serving as horses, you have the recipe for raucous laughter all around, especially when it's all done under the watchful and protective eyes of the omnipresent clowns. Some things have a universal quality to them, don't they?

I'm told by aficionados that the most important ingredient in a successful rodeo is the announcer, who can literally make or break an event. If this is indeed true, then the Kispiox Valley Rodeo is most fortunate to have the services of one Keith Dinwoodie of British Columbia.

And what's not to like? Keith knows the sport inside and out. He has a quick wit and a glib tongue, all wrapped around a million-dollar voice. So with this combination of talents, it's not surprising that Keith, who's also a three-time world auctioning champion, is highly sought after throughout the rodeo world, be it in his native Canada, the U.S. or even Australia. I wonder if they have kangaroo roping contests down under in Oz? Just a thought...

But in the final analysis, it will be memories of the new friendships made that will remain with us when I have even less hair. One such friendship remains forever fresh in my mind.

Exploring the rodeo's periphery rather late Friday evening, I happened upon a grizzled old bloke setting up the barbecue paraphernalia for the huge side of beef that was destined to be consumed long before the last unlucky cowboy was bucked off those scheming Brahmas.

As I was to find out, this type of pit barbecue is an old and exacting science. And if folks expected to eat on time and in great amounts the burden was squarely on his shoulders and his alone. And did he ever revel in that responsibility!

Now he had a captive audience of one and, believe you me, I was not going to escape uninitiated. Accordingly, he quickly launched into a painstakingly precise description of the ins and outs of what constitutes good barbecued beef.

Before we knew it, his soliloquy had taken us to a bitterly cold one a.m.—and it was the first week of June! We had been together for nearly four hours, my newfound friend talking and yours truly listening.

But no matter how interesting, enough is enough and I was about to call it a morning. Then I happened to mention the falling temperatures—a question that was to cost me additional sleep.

Two hours later, he still held my rapt attention as he waxed almost poetically about working, or better still, trying to work with metal in the Yukon's far north in temperatures of minus

40 to 50 degrees below zero Fahrenheit. Did you know that when subjected to such temperature extremes the strongest steel becomes so brittle that it easily snaps when put under the slightest pressure?

He said one of the biggest nightmares under such conditions was the seemingly innocuous event of suffering a flat tire, given the equipment necessary and amount of torque involved. Fascinating stuff from the unlikeliest of sources in the unlikeliest of places and from a friend who never found it necessary to give me his first name, let alone his last!

On a wider scale, I was also gratified with the amount of grass roots friendship existing between the peoples of the United States and Canada. This bond was evident with the playing of both national anthems, "O Canada" and the "Stars and Stripes"—a gesture that both surprised and touched me.

There's no denying that Uncle Sam's long shadow was evident throughout the rodeo, from the corporate sponsorship by such companies as Wrangler Jeans, Budweiser and Coors beers, Brahma Boots, etc., to the aforementioned American rodeo enthusiast ponying up prize money.

But apart from all that, the Kispiox Valley Rodeo will forever be ingrained in my memory because it is one, if not the only, event that passed the Madame LaFarge test with flying colors. You may recall the famous or infamous Madame who, day after grisly day, could be seen sitting and knitting next to one of the busiest guillotines in Paris during the French Revolution.

Suzanne almost never goes anywhere without her crocheting. While she had her more benign implements at the ready the entire weekend, including Sunday, the weekend passed without a single crochet stitch. And, apart from all the other accolades, that's about the highest praise anyone, my wife especially, can bestow on any event.

9

NAME THIS TOWN

I HAVE about 100 residents. None of them pay any local taxes. A foreign currency is legal tender. I have no police force. And up until quite recently my children were educated in a foreign country.

Still can't get it? Hey, don't give up. Here's a couple more hints that might jog your memory. First off: I am located in the United States but outside the Lower Forty-Eight. Secondly, I hold an annual international rodeo with the neighboring foreign town.

To be perfectly honest, this place sounds rather like, at best, something straight out of some surreal novel or, at worst, a bad piece of science fiction. And if you're still grasping at straws, don't feel bad, because if we hadn't visited this place ourselves we'd have been as stumped as you.

The name of the town is Hyder, Alaska, which physically lies a mere two miles from the Canadian town of Stewart. However, in most other ways, Hyder might as well be on an entirely different planet. That's how different it is from Stewart.

Talk to Hyderites and most will tell you flat out that they're in Hyder to escape the bureaucracy, whether it be the American or Canadian variety! They want government out of their lives as much as humanly possible. In fact, that's why most of them moved here in the first place.

With this in mind, they solve their own problems. You break the law in this, "the friendliest little ghost town in Alaska," and you'll find yourself being escorted to the border tout de suite by one or several of the local citizenry who take this unofficial duty quite seriously. If you don't believe me, just try some funny stuff and you'll see what I mean.

Hyder has a Wild West flavor to it, especially with the unpaved streets and in the strongly independent attitude of its citizenry. That's why they ask for as little as possible.

For those of you already intrigued enough to visit, the Stewart-Hyder metroplex (Stewart boasts a population of about 700) is accessed by a spur of the Stewart-Cassiar Highway. To be precise, that spur is named Highway 37A and it begins its 40-mile journey to Stewart at a wide spot in the Stewart-Cassiar Highway called Meziadin Junction.

The visual rewards offered along Highway 37A begin way before you ever reach Stewart or Hyder. About 25 miles in from Stewart-Cassiar there are marvelous close-up views of Bear Glacier, and its accompanying lake.

The summer we were there, some of these views had been temporarily spoiled by the building of this artificially old looking house and outbuildings right at water's edge, all part of the set of a movie soon to be shot there. Not being all that interested, I never bothered to find out if the movie was ever actually filmed there. I assume it was. The only thing I did learn from locals was that the leading man was supposed to be Robert De Niro.

But back to the much more interesting Bear Glacier in all its mystical blueness. While it will be most definitely there long after the film using it as a backdrop is long gone and forgotten, it's also a sad fact that the glacier is retreating at an ac-

47

celerated pace, yet another seeming victim of global warming. The breaking off of varying chunks of this glacier, from huge to rather small pieces, is almost constant—noisy but never boring.

This process is called calving and as we gave it our full, awe-inspired attention, Bear Glacier was indeed calving to a fare-thee-well, with the lake formed at its base just chocka-block full of said calves of all shapes and sizes.

While Bear Glacier seemed quite grandiose in size and scope, it's said to pale in comparison to a nearby relative, the Salmon Glacier, purported to be the world's fifth largest. Alas, I'm compelled to use qualifying words here, having had the misfortune of not actually seeing it for myself.

Every now and then on such travels, one experiences disappointments of various magnitudes, while learning to roll, no matter how reluctantly, with the scenic punches. And continuing with this pugilistic metaphor, not being able to view the Salmon up close and personal, so to speak, equated with being pummeled mercilessly by the likes of a Mohammed Ali for 12 long and painful rounds.

We were right there! We could even see the road that would take us to the Salmon. The only problem was that the British Columbia government had a policy (or at least it did when we were there) of not plowing the road leading to the glacier, rather leaving Mother Nature to deal with it in her own sweet time. And due to heavy snows that winter it was estimated that cars would be prevented from getting to within viewing distance of Salmon until mid-July.

We just didn't have the three weeks to wait around for the big melt. So not being ones to give up easily, we heeded the advice of locals who told us to drive up the road as far as the snow line, wherever that was. And then the only decision to be made would be whether or not to turn around. All this made sense to us and sounded perfectly safe and error proof.

I must admit that while quite pleasant, the trip took on a rather surreal quality. We found ourselves hoping against hope that some miracle would occur, allowing the impossible. But just when we were getting our hopes up regarding Mother Nature's generosity, we rounded a sharp bend and there was the heavy snow line piled up across the entire road.

Oh well, it was fun dreaming we could fool the experts and make it all the way to the mighty Salmon Glacier. But in our heart of hearts we knew it was never really in the cards! Besides, even though we didn't get to see the Salmon, the snow on the road had retreated beyond the entrances to some interesting abandoned mines, including one called the Granduc. So it was by no means a wasted effort.

In addition, there was another important reason for attempting this trip, besides the pure adventure of just going and doing something others might not. Early on down the small narrow road, we had passed by a wide spot called the Fish Creek Wildlife Viewing Area.

I know, I know, many of you non-fishing types just couldn't care less at this point. But before you leave us, mentally or physically, consider this: each and every year thousands upon thousands of seemingly sane folks from the four corners of the globe descend upon this small, rather innocuous, platform out in the bush with a single goal in mind.

All are in search of "the" perfect photo of a black bear or a bald eagle. But not just any garden variety bear or eagle. No sirree, they also have to be participating in a specific activity to boot. These black bears and bald eagles must be at water's edge or slightly above it, all cadging free meals of Chum and Pink salmon as they return up this specific stream to spawn.

So now you see why, between July and September, this relatively small spot is inundated by droves of folks, all determined to take one of those prize-winning photos. But our string of less-than-good luck was holding and we were about three weeks too early for this annual salmon feast! We keep telling ourselves there's always another time.

While in the thriving metropolis of Hyder, we were comfortably ensconced in the town's lone RV park, called Camp Run Amuck. Don't you love the name? Suzie, the woman running the place back then, was a virtual gold mine of information. During our rather animated, but bug-shortened, conversation she regaled us with story after story about the considerable lore and uniqueness that is Hyder.

Indeed there's much to like about the folks of Hyder. Above all else, I admire their pioneer spirit and their determination to protect this hard-fought and nurtured independence from the clutches of the ever-encroaching state bureaucratic tentacles. At times this has meant turning down services sorely needed, knowing full well these came with too high a price tag in terms of personal liberties and freedoms that they treasure above all else.

Sure, by Lower Forty-Eight standards, the good folks of Hyder are seen by some as a rather rough and ready lot with highly questionable mental quotients. All that aside, the majority of folks living here are salt-of-the-earth types with a basic sense of decency, hard work and generosity almost ingrained in them. But make no mistake about it—they are, above all else, a tough breed because the fact remains that the weak or unprepared just don't survive long in such hostile surroundings.

And I know how terribly tough and debilitating Hyder's hostile surroundings can be from first hand experience. Just imagine how close I came to a complete nervous breakdown when a thorough search of Hyder's few stores failed to locate my favorite chocolate bar and soft drink!

Thoroughly shaken and totally demoralized, I knew right

then, in concrete terms, the extent to which the folks of Hyder suffered. I also knew that if I were to stand any chance of regaining my emotional and mental equilibrium, it was time for the Maughans to make for the Canadian border and in all due haste.

After all, and I'm sure you'd agree, there's only so much deprivation any one man can be expected to endure! Talk about cruel and unbearable punishment. This town of Hyder really knows how to dish it out!

10

OUR SECRET

I'M SURE you can keep a secret. After all, what's so hard about keeping your lips sealed, right? But just to make sure—after all, we can't be too careful in such matters—raise your right hand, place the other on your religion's sacred scriptures and repeat after me: on my word of honor, I pledge not to divulge to a living soul the secret I'm about to be told.

Great. Now I feel better about letting the proverbial cat out of the bag. After all, who else will ever know about our secret except, maybe, all those other folks also reading this book. But I'm sure we can trust them as well.

With that little piece of business taken care of, let me tell you about what I consider to be one of British Columbia's best kept scenic secrets—the Valley of the Stikine River. Making this almost magical place extra special is the fact that on most days you'll have its entire physical splendor pretty much to yourself.

Of course I can't guarantee that every now and then you won't be joined by a few other adventurous souls willing to take the blinkers off and divert their attention away from the mad dash northwards to Alaska. But even if you have to share the road every once and awhile, there's generally plenty of room for everyone!

But like most things worthwhile, the Stikine Valley doesn't give itself away cheaply or without appropriate effort and risk. To put it another way, you'll have to work for your pleasure and only the smaller rigs of the 25 feet or less variety should even attempt the adventure. But, believe me, the rewards along the way will more than repay the effort.

What's that? Oh, you say you don't quite believe me. Fine. If you must persist in being a "doubting Thomas" maybe you'll have more faith in no less an authority than The Milepost. Here's what that "bible" of travel guides to the northwestern region has to say about this particular stretch of road: "Telegraph Creek Road has some steep sections and several sets of steep switch backs; it is not recommended for trailers or large RVs...DRIVE CAREFULLY! Use caution when road is wet or icy. Watch for rocks and mud." Enough said.

The 80-plus miles of testing, twisting, mostly gravel road that runs through, down and around the Stikine River and Valley is also called Highway 51 for all those map checkers among you.

There's little to betray the scope of the adventure ahead when Telegraph Creek Road innocuously forks off near the town center of Dease Lake, which sits at the 300 mile mark as you travel north along the Stewart-Cassiar Highway.

I'd love to be able to tell you that you can follow the Stikine clear down to where it empties into the ocean just north of the Alaskan town of Wrangell. But you can't. Unfortunately, Telegraph Creek Road ends at Glenora, leaving the mighty Stikine to continue meandering south southwest through British Columbia until it eventually enters Alaska and opens into the Pacific Ocean. The Stikine River rises in the Stikine Mountains more than 300 miles away in northwestern British Columbia.

Judging by the size of the dot on our map, we fully expected Glenora to be... well, something. But it's not. If I've only succeeded in thoroughly confusing you, let me explain.

I know you've heard of and have most likely visited several so-called ghost towns in your time. They're scattered all over the western United States and rightly attract hordes of tourists. Even though, by their very definition, no one still lives in these towns, derelict buildings at least remain, marking the place where folks once lived, loved and died. Not so with Glenora.

Telegraph Creek Road just sort of ends, with little more than a haphazard-looking parking area among the trees lining the river to form a final, rather nondescript, cul de sac. Folks use the Stikine as their own personal marine highway in order to reach properties further down the river. They simply tie their boats up to the bank, hop into their trucks, which are permanently parked there, and continue their journey into town, most usually Dease Lake.

In fact, there's very little else to mark the previous existence of any town named Glenora. Oh, when we scoured the area during our four days of boondocking there, we did manage to find scattered evidence of previous habitation. But these derelict buildings were few and far between and not apparent to the casual observer. In other words, you really have to want to find them!

But let the record show that Glenora was, for a brief time, something of a boomtown in the 1860s. At its zenith, during an abortive attempt to build a railroad to the Yukon, it boasted a population in excess of 10,000. If the name sounds familiar, you may recall it was that very same Yukon that was attracting quite a crowd due to the abundance of a certain valuable metal being found there.

The reason for this sudden interest in Glenora and the larger town of Telegraph Creek, which is about 12 miles upstream, lay in the fact that they were directly on what was called the "All Canada" route to the Klondike gold fields in the Yukon. It stood to reason that the faster you could get to the gold fields, the better your chances of striking it rich. So competing routes, all touting that they were the fastest (but not necessarily the safest) were being devised by the entrepreneurs making money off those madly streaming north seeking their fortune.

For those interested in such things, this particular route involved navigating the Stikine to Glenora or Telegraph Creek, then traveling up the so-called Stikine-Teslin Trail to gold fields in the area around Atlin and, of course, the Klondike. And it's estimated that about 5,000 gold-fevered men made their mad dash via this route.

Nowadays the Stikine River and Valley hold a different kind of promise. About half way along Telegraph Creek Road after leaving Dease Lake you begin to wind up into and through one spectacular canyon after another. The road literally clings to the side of the cliffs. And just to make things even more challenging, two grades of 18 percent and one of 20 are thrown into the mix for good measure. Add several blind hairpin curves and exhilarating switch backs and you have a driving experience challenging enough to thoroughly test the most skilled off-road driver.

And as there's only the one road in and out, an 18 or 20 percent up or downhill grade on the way in turns into an entirely different challenge heading out. I thought I had seen some steep inclines in my albeit limited RVing life, but these were truly mind blowing. I can remember being so thankful for a dry track and powerful lower gears in our 2000 Ford F-350 turbo diesel dually super cab truck.

If you're expecting all sorts of technical mumbo jumbo about how the truck performed as well as she did, forget it. All I can tell you is that Bridget, with nearly 4,000 pounds of Bigfoot truck camper on her back, went up and down those grades like a hot knife through butter. Heading up or going down, it didn't matter. I just put her in low, whispered in her ear very reassuringly, and ever so slowly but surely she did the rest, never missing a beat. After all, Bridget is definitely one lady built for power and comfort, not for speed!

The rugged and isolated Stikine River and
Valley in northern British Columbia.

As I said earlier, the Stikine River is in the process of carving itself a canyon that will eventually rival that of the Grand Canyon. Admittedly, right now that image takes a wee bit of imagination, but in a mere million years or so I guarantee you'll see what I mean!

And adding to the splendor was the fact that we had the drive all to ourselves. Thank goodness, as in several tight spots I would have been at great pains to back up—and that's the weakest part of my driving repertoire, or so says my Suzanne.

In fact, during the entire five-hour trip to Glenora (an average of about 15 miles an hour) we saw only seven other vehicles. And all encounters mercifully occurred during the scattered wide spots in the road. Talk about good karma!

Between Dease Lake and Telegraph Creek there are only two settlements of any size whatsoever. At the first one, Tahtlan, First Nation people eke out a living of sorts by fishing, though you couldn't prove that by us, as the village seemed quite deserted.

It was these very same Tahtlans who once supplemented their income by breeding a very special, courageous species of dog. Rather short in stature but stout of heart, these fierce and totally fearless dogs readily hunted and attacked bears. That's right, you read correctly—bears! This was their raison d'etre, if you will.

But now the Tahtlan bear dogs, as they were known and recognized by the Canadian Kennel Club, are thought to be extinct, leaving folks like us to ponder whether their fate was caused by a genetic breakdown of one sort or the other or one too many of the dogs coming out on the losing end against a seemingly vastly superior adversary!

Telegraph Creek is the only place vaguely resembling a town... and then just. It boasts one gas station, complete with mechanic, a church or two, a few houses scattered hither and yon, and a combination cafe/grocery store/lodge/river guide center with the colorful name of The Stikine River Song. During our ramblings we've visited several establishments like this, from Kenya to Thailand, and we never fail to wonder how the proprietors manage to make a go of it financially. In the case of The Stikine River Song, one can hardly believe they get enough trade from adventurous RVers like us.

I was told, however, that they get occasional river trade from Americans on river safari from Wrangell. Apart from that rather iffy source of clientele, heavy reliance has had to be placed on the seasonal supply of avid fishermen matching wits and skill with the river's legendary migratory salmon population.

After a day of such demanding driving there was no way that we weren't going to sit a spell somewhere, regroup, and listen to the quiet. So 12 miles and a 90-minute drive later, Glenora experienced a population boom of two when the Maughans dropped anchor in a wide meadow smack dab in the center of the ghost town.

But as we were soon to realize, literally millions of other squatters had already taken up residence. What's more, they seemed downright pleased that two interlopers had decided to join them. In fact, several swarms of these ferocious, voracious and very noisy mosquitoes paid us a social call, telling us they were planning on inviting us to join them for dinner with the two of us as the main course!

Thank goodness for screens which, at times, seemed in imminent danger of caving in under the sheer weight of the number of winged well-wishers pressing in to welcome us to the neighborhood. But happily, the screens held and the cacophony of our mosquito serenaders was soon more than drowned out by the almost tinkling sound of aspen leaves rustling in a newly sprung breeze.

This island of tranquility was to be our home for four glorious days, during which the solitude and total isolation more than repaid us for the arduous effort of getting there. Increasingly, we're finding it's getting harder and harder to discover such idyllic places—places where the time of day rarely matters. But we had indeed succeeded in finding such a place—a place smack dab in a town that no longer exists and at the end of a road that led to nowhere.

11

ESCAPE FROM
PETERSBURG

No, it's not the sequel to the movie "Escape From Alcatraz." About everyone is familiar with that film. For the uninitiated, it's the one in which a group of determined inmates attempt to do what no other prisoner has ever managed to accomplish— make it to shore safely from this maximum security prison surrounded by the treacherous currents of San Francisco Bay.

Rather, this real life drama is played out hundreds of miles almost due north of "the city by the bay" on northern British Columbia's mighty Stikine River. And instead of Sean Connery playing the title role, Escape From Petersburg features Mike and Debby, two friends banding together to escape something equally fearsome—rain. Yep, you read correctly, rain, seemingly endless, rain!

Now wipe that quizzical smirk off your face and hear me out. Consider this: the Petersburg Mike and Debby are so desperate to vacate, if only for a few precious hours, is not Saint Petersburg of Florida fun-in-the-sun fame.

Rather, this particular Petersburg, minus the Saint, is a regular port of call on the inside passage along Alaska's Panhandle region. Apart from boasting the largest home-based halibut fleet in Alaska, Petersburg's other, more dubious, claim to fame is the fact that it can get as much as 150 inches of liquid sunshine every year, ranking it among the state's leaders in that regard.

A yearly dousing of 150 inches of mostly rain, with some snow thrown in just for fun, might not seem all that heavy to some. Why to some of us old Africa hands, that amount, and more, can and does fall regularly in the tropical rainy season, which lasts as little as two or three months. But that's the deluge variety, as in a totally-drenched-in-just-a-few-seconds-if-caught-out-without-an-umbrella sort of rain.

Petersburg, for the most part, has the maddening, drizzly variety also referred to as "soft" in far-off Ireland, where, I dare say, the locals also know a wee bit about the wet stuff!

Debby put it best: "It's enough to drive us crazy. Many days it's nonstop rain. Not the pouring down kind, mind you, just that relentless drizzle that seemingly goes on for day after interminable day, slowly driving you to distraction and planning any sort of escape possible!"

So what to do? You're right. You could pack your bags and relocate to Death Valley, California, or some other place where umbrellas need not apply. But if you earn a pretty good living as an experienced salmon fisherman like Mike, that's not really a viable option. Besides, as soggy as it is, Petersburg is home, complete with everything associated with it.

So you do the next best thing. Whenever you're on the verge of going stark, raving mad, you simply load Debby and yourself into one of your boats and point her bow (the boat's, not Debby's) up the Stikine River into Canada until you reach sunshine. And you keep going even if it takes you 175 miles to do so!

Suzanne and I caught up with our two sun worshippers

contentedly flipping a frisbee around our heretofore private campground in the ghost town of Glenora, the last possible destination along Telegraph Creek Road, which parallels the Stikine. They readily admitted that the outdoor exercise was merely a necessity to dry out a bit and to reacquaint themselves with what sunshine actually felt like! They also noted that sunshine was said to be good for getting rid of mildew.

Mike and Debby allowed that the almost constant precipitation is bad enough in the spring and summer, when it stays light until late in the evening. But, they said, it really starts driving them bonkers in the late autumn and winter, when the drizzly conditions are compounded by darkness descending upon them at around three in the afternoon.

All this has given me a great idea. I think I'll advise our daughter to set up her psychology practice in Petersburg. It seems a perfect spot for such a practice, despite the fact that it boasts a population of less than 3,400. After all, in that profession it's need, not numbers!

And, besides that, Mike and Debby assured us that when the sun does put in an occasional appearance, Petersburg and the surrounding countryside are most worthwhile to visit, especially if you like fishing and spectacular scenery. And who doesn't?

Naturally, when we asked these two Petersburgers where they like to go to reconnect with their sanity, we fully expected to hear them mention logical places like San Diego, Acapulco or maybe even Hawaii. Nope, wrong on all three counts. Their favorite vacation destination—get this—is that dry-as-a-bone spot, Seattle! Go figure! Maybe the rain down there is different. Could it be it's not wet?

Mike and Debby's ultimate destination on this particular quest for the golden orb was the Stikine River Song Cafe and Lodge in Telegraph Creek, the only place to stay in this town of any size upriver from Alaska. There they planned to rendez-vous with two other sun-seeking fugitives from Petersburg and get a meal and a room, before making the trek back to wet and soggy Petersburg, just in time to trudge through the puddles Monday morning on their way to work.

In talking to the owners of the Stikine River Song, we learned that Mike and Debby are only two of a constant stream of American seasonal visitors from Petersburg and the neighboring Alaskan town of Wrangell. Yep, you guessed it—Wrangell also gets more than its fair share of rain.

Not only do the American visitors get to escape the dreaded rain, but they do so in a recognized Canadian Heritage build-ing dating back to 1898, which was first used as a trading post by the famous Hudson Bay Company. In fact, the Stikine River Song Cafe and Lodge is located in an area of Telegraph Creek that we were told was little changed since gold rush days.

But talk about fact sometimes being stranger than fiction. Do you want to know the upshot of this story? Of course you do. Well, shortly after Mike and Debby's arrival, several days of glorious sunshine were suddenly replaced by rain. And when I say rain, I mean rain that would have made the tropics proud! It literally poured down, day after foggy and soggy day.

Now, trust me, those who know me will verify that I'm not a vengeful fellow. In fact, I consider myself to be quite sane and rational. But, having said that, I believe every person has his or her breaking point! So I ask you, in your opinion, would it be a punishable offense to hog tie a couple of rain makers in their own boat and let the Stikine River gently and safely float them back to Petersburg or to whatever soggy place they came from?

If apprehended, my defense would be quite simple. I'd merely plead temporary insanity and throw myself on the mercy of the court, confident that no jury of my peers would ever convict me! After all, wouldn't they agree that, given the circumstances, desperate measures were necessary to end what could only be described as Mike and Debby's "rain" of terror!

12

CANADA'S DANIEL BOONE

YOU READ about people like him. But, in your wildest dreams, you never really think you'll ever meet one of his ilk face to face.

You may be wondering why. Well these types of folks have been, for the most part, relegated to history books where the stuff of myth and legend intertwines with real life, good and bad. But now here he stood, this Daniel Boone look alike, so close that I was tempted to reach out and touch him just to make sure he was real and not merely a figment of my imagination.

His name is Laurie Brock and his road to what he'd consider as civilization is the Stikine River.

You see, apart from the road that begins in this ghost town of Glenora and runs through Telegraph Creek and eventually to Dease Lake on the Stewart-Cassiar Highway, there is no other road, period. This is it!

Suzanne and I met Laurie shortly after his jet boat (an obvious euphemism by the rate of speed his boat was traveling) pulled into the riverbank. As he was cutting off the boat's homemade diesel engine, he noticed us upstream and gave us a friendly wave.

Laurie, of unremarkable height and build, had just motored four miles up from his homestead where he, wife Sarah and 11-month-old live in total seclusion, having literally hacked their plot of ground out of the wilderness.

Come to find out that Laurie had joined us in Glenora to check on his truck which he and his fellow downstream neighbors leave by the bank in "private parking spaces." Again these "parking spaces" were decidedly homemade, located as they were randomly in and among trees lining the river.

Being city slickers at heart, we asked Laurie if he was worried about his truck being vandalized, seeing it was parked so far from his place. I wish you could have seen his reaction. Talk about a look speaking volumes! When he had regained his composure, he answered with a succinct, "No."

Unlike most of us, Laurie knew his neighbors quite well—all four of them! Most, he explained, lived on the other side of the Stikine so the little socializing they did do had to be done via boat, except in the winter time, that is, when the river froze over and they could walk!

Laurie's boat draws only five inches, which is fine because the Stikine was at high water right then. But, as Laurie explained, the level drops precipitously come April when the ice begins to break up.

Continuing our informal education, Laurie told us that when the Stikine is really high it's about 200 yards wide. But at low water, he said, that distance is reduced to less than 30 yards!

Laurie had come to "town" to change the oil in his truck as he and his family had a funeral to attend in the next day or so. He and Sarah had bought their piece of wilderness about six years ago and had lived there alone until being joined by Melody.

The small one-room cabin that came with the land had been big enough until Melody's arrival. Now Laurie was building a 30 by 40 foot two-story house entirely from local forest materials, using only his own labor.

He does have a joiner, a lathe and all the necessary tools that he powers by means of twenty 12-volt deep cycle batteries. These, in turn, are kept topped up by a diesel-powered generator. All told, Laurie reckons it takes one gallon of diesel for three hours of power! I wonder how many of us would know what it takes to power our homes?

In fact, Laurie told us that his one major expense is fuel, which he keeps in two 500 gallon storage tanks, one gas and the other diesel. These are on the property of a friend close by the town of Telegraph Creek, which sports a population of 300, give or take a moose or two!

So when he needs fuel, up the Stikine he motors, hops in his pickup and drives the five or so miles to the place where he fills up his jerry cans from his storage tanks that are filled once a year by a truck from the city of Terrace, nearly 500 miles to the south. And we think it's rough having to go down to the corner gas station to fill up!

But Laurie says he never fuels up without combining that chore with a visit to Telegraph Creek to pick up the limited supplies they need and to check his mail. But they need few "store bought" supplies. In the spring and summer they grow their own vegetables, mainly corn, tomatoes and cucumbers. Protein is supplied by salmon from the river and moose from the forest.

Laurie's income comes from occasional boat hires up and down the Stikine and winter trapping of marten, mink, wolverine, lynx, etc., which he sells to an American fur buyer in Ottawa. For a man with so many wilderness skills and ingenuity Laurie is remarkably self-effacing and modest. But isn't that generally the way? In fact, if people start bragging about themselves I get the distinct need to put some distance between us!

Those boat hires take Laurie downstream across the American border to the small Alaskan towns of Wrangell and Petersburg. But not to worry about customs, he says, it's quite an informal system they've worked out. Just leave your name and telephone number on their answering service to let the custom folks know you're in town! Wow, wouldn't it be nice if other border crossings were that easy and relaxed?

But if you want to see what Laurie's really made of—the fire in his belly, if you will—just suggest that he move into town and begin living a "normal" life! Change his lifestyle? Never, he says, because, as he puts it, bureaucrats and city folk are just not his cup of tea, present company excepted of course!

Standing there talking to Laurie Brock, it seemed clear that he would have fit in comfortably during an era when the Stikine River and Valley were used as little more than convenient conduits to reaching the riches that lay further north in the Yukon gold fields. But further conversation revealed one fundamental difference between Laurie and those thousands upon thousands of gold-fevered men. While they viewed this area as merely a necessary evil along the way to fame and fortune, to Laurie and Sarah Brock this valley represents their entire world—a world to be left only for very special occasions, such as a funeral or the birth of a child.

Although we never met Laurie's wife, Sarah, I could tell from his description that she not only loves their lifestyle, but has also cultivated the necessary skills to more than hold up her end of the bargain. To listen to Laurie, she does it all. Among her many talents, Sarah sews most of their clothes, tends their extensive vegetable gardens and, during the relatively short spring and summer growing seasons, she makes sure they won't go hungry that coming winter by laying by a store of surplus vegetables, salmon and moose.

As if that weren't enough to keep her busy, Sarah fully intends to home school Melody, something almost all of their neighbors also do. Additional children have not been ruled out and if and when they do arrive they'll be delivered at home if there are no complications.

Laurie and Sarah are from the British Columbia city of Vanderhoof, which lies about 600 miles south southeast of their place on the Stikine. And even though they spent six and a half years there, Vanderhoof might as well be 60,000 miles away.

"We're here to stay," Laurie told us emphatically, "because this place gets under your skin to the point that you never want to be anywhere else." And, you know, standing there on the banks of that magnificent river, surrounded by such incredible beauty and solitude, we couldn't have agreed more.

13

INTO EACH LIFE...

... A little rain must fall. Aw heck, that little nugget of home-spun wisdom might apply to some folks. But, if the truth be known, when precipitation hit the Maughans that June day of 2001, it came in the form of a relentless, torrential downpour, nearly drowning all our RVing dreams in the process!

Like most people out there enjoying the full-time RVing lifestyle, we complacently figured that accidents and other bad things only happened to other persons. You know what I mean as we've all had the exact same feeling.

Does this sound all too familiar? You come across some sort of accident involving an RV. You feel a genuine sense of sympathy, empathy, sorrow, dread, call it what you will, in your heart. But you can't help but feel a certain relief, no matter how tiny or fleeting, that you're not the ones going through the agony, heartache and torture. To put it crassly—better them than you!

Suzanne and I plead guilty to having had very similar feelings from time to time. That doesn't make us bad people. It just makes us human. So feel free to join the "I'm glad that's not us" club without feeling you have to beat yourself up mentally.

So, seemingly secure, we were hardly prepared for the utter shock and devastation when disaster struck in the form of a bad electrical fire—a conflagration that came that close to burning up our camper. The "it-always-happens-to-the-other-guy" event occurred as we were winding up four days of glorious, totally isolated, free camping in the ghost town of Glenora, on the banks of the Stikine River in northern British Columbia.

The weather having turned sour, we decided to wind our way back to the town of Dease Lake on the Stewart-Cassiar Highway. Our immediate destination, however, was much closer—the tiny settlement of Telegraph Creek, some 10 miles or so up the dirt road, where we planned to stop at the Stikine River Song Cafe for some souvenirs, good food and even better conversation. After all, it had been four whole days with no one else for this flaming extrovert to talk to except my wife. And I could see her eyes were beginning to glaze over!

We'd only been on the road for a few minutes when for some inexplicable reason we still haven't quite fathomed, Suzanne asked me to stop so she could take some video shots of the scenery with her camcorder. What scenery, I asked derisively, referring to the foggy, rainy conditions almost totally blotting out what admittedly was a scenic wonder when the sun was shining.

Reluctantly, and with much grumbling under my breath, I remember stopping for what I considered to be little more than an exercise in picture-taking futility. No sooner had Suzanne got out and walked towards the rear of the camper than she came racing back yelling that the smoke detector was blaring away.

Of course, Mr. Know It All was sure it was merely a malfunctioning alarm clock choosing this inopportune time to act up yet again. But my wife insisted (read that nagged) that I get my butt in gear and go back there and investigate.

Thank goodness she did because, when I finally opened the back door, I was greeted by a pall of thick, white, terribly acrid and, for lack of a more descriptive word, electrical-type smoke. After the initial shock and an acute feeling of "this is not happening to us" subsided, I sprang into action.

I wish at this point I could tell you that my vast knowledge of all things mechanical and electrical came to the fore. If I did, like Pinocchio, my already sizable nose would get much bigger still. Pure and simple, as a technical person I'm an excellent radio broadcaster! You get the picture.

After doing many things I later learned were of no use whatsoever, I suddenly had the bright idea (from where I still have no clue) to disconnect one of the battery cables, thus breaking the circuit. Talk about blind sows accidentally finding an acorn now and then! Inadvertently, I had stumbled on just the right thing to do!

Opening up the battery compartment and then disconnecting one of the battery cables, I immediately saw the cause of the problem. Duh, an Einstein I'm not, but this was obvious to even this mechanical genius! One of wires had shorted out somewhere along the line, frying all the accompanying wires throughout the camper along with it.

What a mess! And one accompanied by an acrid, toxic and highly pungent stink that can be imagined only by those who've suffered the same fate.

But at least the truck was still in one piece. Fortunately, I had had an isolator installed, effectively curtailing any possibility of us inadvertently siphoning off vital energy from our two 12-volt truck batteries. As it was explained later, the truck was saved because as the short reached the isolator its fuse had blown, preventing any further damage.

Thank goodness for small miracles, as things would have been decidedly much worse if our truck engine had been burned up as well. But it wasn't, and as a result we were able to at least limp back into Dease Lake (a seemingly endless drive of 80 miles) to better gather our wits and to begin making the seemingly thousand and one telephone calls that suddenly had to be made.

At this point, all we knew was that something terribly wrong had happened to the camper wiring and that our entire Alaska adventure was in dire jeopardy of also going up in smoke, if you'll pardon the unfortunate play on words!

Indeed, the next couple of days were filled with endless stressful reminders of how close we had in fact come to losing it all. The two most important calls were made to camper manufacturers, Bigfoot, and to our insurance company. We needed guidance and we needed it from calm and collected folks who, in a sense, were no strangers to such situations.

But, in hindsight, possibly an equally important call was the one to a local electrical mechanic who, after a thorough examination, confirmed our worst fears: the camper's entire electrical wiring system had been burned to a crisp. Even our camper's 12-volt deep cycle battery had not been spared!

But for all its shock value, the mechanic's demonstrated expertise, unvarnished and never sugar coated, served to give us back something badly shaken ever since the fire—our confidence and peace of mind. So with the knowledge that all remaining potential energy sources in the camper had now been disabled we were able to turn our attention to the next major job at hand—a 500 mile, one-day trip to Bigfoot's designated RV repair shop, Fireweed RV, in Yukon's capital city of Whitehorse.

The ultimate shocking revelations supplied by the Whitehorse Fire Chief and the Yukon's Territorial Fire Marshal surprised us all. Not only were they able to pinpoint the fire's exact genesis but also, working under a cloak of secrecy after ordering us all from the room, they succeeded in recreating the entire scenario directly preceding the fire.

It seems that under the constant downward vibration applied by our propane tanks, one of the electrical wires eventually cracked and arced, nearly sending Bridget and her owners to the happy hunting grounds! We can joke about it now. But suffice it to say, ever since then we've never been able to look at an accident involving another recreational vehicle in quite the same detached way.

Gone is this blasé, self-centered notion that bad things only happen to other folks. Now we knew better—much, much better. And we had a badly fire-and-smoke-damaged truck camper to prove it!

14

A RAINY DAY IN
WHITEHORSE

You're in Whitehorse, Yukon. It's a rainy, thoroughly yukky, type of day—that sort of day when no one in his or her right mind would be caught dead out of doors. And to make matters even more desperate, you're suffering from a really severe case of cabin, or, more to the point, RV fever.

So what to do? You ask yourself what things do so-called "normal" folks get up to indoors to one: stay in out of the wet; and two: get away from their recreational vehicle for a few hours? No, that's not a trick question but I will tell you that the key word is "normal," whatever the heck that is!

I've often wondered—is "normal" what you are or what you think other folks are? And if each and every one of us is thinking the other folks are normal, are there, in fact, any normal folks on this earth? Aah, life's many conundrums!

After all, like most capital cities, Whitehorse has much to offer both indoors and out, so it's not like you're stuck for ideas. For starters, there's a full-service library downtown very accommodating to visitors.

They have an entire room devoted to the Yukon and its

famous gold rush, if that's what gets you up in the morning. But if it's not, not to worry, as the Whitehorse Public Library is loaded with just about everything that might tickle your fancy in the way of books.

Want something a little less cerebral? How about a visit to the Yukon Beringia Interpretive Centre, where, according to its ads, ice-age science and myth reign supreme, as does a huge skeleton of a woolly mammoth.

If that's a mammoth turnoff, there's always the Qwanlin Mall, where you can shop 'til you drop and wile away the hours in the process. I don't know about you, but I like to browse in the smaller boutique-type stores. And if you share that interest, then the Qwanlin Mall will suit you to a tee.

Still not your style? Then why not try a visit to the Whitehorse Rapids Fishway. If you're there at just the right time, during the spawning run between mid-July and early September, you'll most likely get to see the Chinook or King Salmon using the man-made fishway to get around the Yukon Energy Corporation Hydroelectric dam. And to make sure you get an up close and personal look at each Chinook as it continues its epic journey to its original spawning grounds, the fish are channeled through glass-covered runs.

This system also serves a much more practical purpose. During the spawning run, volunteers sit in front of the glass windows counting each fish as it goes by in order to get a accurate count of that year's run. And this valuable information is, in turn, passed along upriver.

It's fascinating stuff and, again, it's indoors! And while you're there, why don't you follow my lead and buy one of their distinctive baseball caps featuring, what else, a colorful King Salmon. It'll be a great conversation starter and you know the money is going to a good cause.

I could go on and on but you get the picture: if you get

soaked in Whitehorse it's because you're a masochist or just plain crazy!

While all the above are surely attractive diversions on a rainy day, we were fortunate to stumble across an event that was to prove both fascinating and quite illuminating. As we were stumbling and grumbling around trying to figure out what to do in out of the rain, we happened upon a small flyer that simply announced there was to be a dog show. And as luck would have it, that very day!

Don't ask me why this registered some sort of responsive chord in both of us, but for some reason it did. So off we went to a large facility on a nearby campus.

The dog show was being held by the Yukon Kennel Club— an event they had been holding yearly since it was organized in 1970. And to add a little extra spice they had invited their Alaskan equivalent to join them. Nothing better than a little international rivalry and competition to spice things up, eh?

Now you have to understand that we are neophytes when it comes to dog shows. In fact we've never even as much as owned a dog during our 40-plus years of married life, preferring cats instead.

So talk about being innocents abroad. But this lack of expertise didn't get in the way of our becoming totally engrossed as we wandered from area to area talking to American and Canadian entrants and officials alike, as they prepared for the big day ahead.

The one good thing about being newcomers is not knowing if you're violating some time-honored taboo. For instance, if there were an unwritten rule in the dog show world against talking to folks before a show, then we would most certainly have been in deep doo-doo.

But as everyone reacted most kindly and with total cooperation, we just assumed we were fine and not ruffling any feathers, or hair, for that matter. So along our merry way we went.

It's amazing how much gossip you can hear and how much you can learn about the inner machinations by just sitting and keep your ears peeled. As with any highly competitive and passionate endeavor, dog shows are not without their intrigues, petty and otherwise. And the Yukon Dog Show was surely no exception.

We heard how certain judges were said to favor certain specific breeds, the logistics of how best to prepare a pooch mentally and physically, and the strategy of how best to present your charge to the respective judges. We even eavesdropped on a rather erudite and heartfelt discussion regarding what shampoo works best on what breed. Fascinating stuff, I kid you not.

But the best was still to come. And talk about serendipity. After a morning's judging that seemed to fly by, it was time to chow down at the school cafeteria, overlooking the main hall. As one would imagine, things were a wee bit crowded, so eating alone was out of the question. Accordingly, we were soon joined at our table by a rather bland looking fellow.

Never one to turn down an opportunity to meet someone new, I immediately struck up a conversation, while being careful not to give away any of my thoughts and opinions on the morning's proceedings. Good move, because the chap turned out to be one of the show's top judges and one of the world's leading authorities on the Basenji, which I was soon to learn was a unique Rhodesian breed, along with the Rhodesian Ridgeback.

What followed was a fascinating but necessarily brief conversation on dog judging, with me peppering him with questions faster than he could answer them. To put it mildly, we struck a chord, so much so that he invited us to watch him judge certain breeds, while giving us a thumbnail sketch of what he looked for in each one, some of the common failings of the breed, and how he separated the excellent from the good and the not-so-good to finally crown a champion.

It was as if a brand new world had been opened up to us, not that we were now experts by any stretch of the imagination. But now we would be able to observe more discerningly and possibly, just possibly, detect the characteristics that separated champ from chump.

For the rest of the day we stalked him as he went about his duties. And it soon became apparent that his celebrity had preceded him, as he was clearly given many of the more prestigious judging duties.

After the end of the show, we joined our new friend for a sort of unofficial post mortem. It was then that we learned the actual extent of his standing in the dog judging world community, in general, and in the world of Basenjis, in particular.

Slowly but surely this self-effacing man revealed that in the next six months he had been invited to judge in such far away and diverse places as Spain, Huntsville, Alabama, and Australia. In fact, he told us that his judging duties generally take him away from his home in the Canadian capital of Ottawa for several months each year.

We exchanged business cards with no real expectations of staying in touch. But we did. And now we're the proud owners of a couple of his texts detailing not only the origins of the Basenji breed, but also the seemingly endless number of nuances that go into judging this fascinating breed and every other one as well.

So the next time you're looking for something to do outside your RV on one of those rainy miserable days, think about what "normal" people would do. And then go do something entirely different.

For as we found out, it's simply amazing what can happen when all you want to do is get indoors and stay out of the rain in Whitehorse, Yukon. Or in any other place, for that matter.

15

DO YOU HEAR IT?

HEAR WHAT, you say? C'mon, try a little harder. Listen closely. You might have to strain those ears of yours a little but trust me, the effort will be more than worth it. Eureka, you've done it! The sound, you say, is coming through loud and clear!

What's that you say? Mmm... I thought you'd have that reaction. But so what if the late Luciano Pavarotti had nothing to worry about. And enough already about the value of our day jobs! After all, what do you want for nothing, your money back?

Hey, even if we do concede the accuracy of your rather negative assessment of our vocal stylings, Suzanne and yours truly really couldn't care less. Why? Well, when we belt out Willie Nelson's famous hit, On the Road Again, we're singing it strictly for ourselves and for no other living soul.

But why all the warbling? Well, a little more than two weeks after arriving in Whitehorse, Yukon, (16 days, but who's counting) our beloved truck camper, Bridget, is finally back in one piece again and ready for more adventures. At long last, the fine, competent and accommodating folks at Fireweed RV (you always praise them after a job's done, right?) have actually finished repairing the last of the damage caused by the electrical fire that threatened to consume not only our home on wheels, but also the two of us in the process.

But before actually getting "on the road again" we first had to do what seemed to be a million and one things. Right off the bat, a large bubble (the tire folks in these parts call it a chipmunk) was found in the side wall of one of the front tires. So off we went to the local Ford dealer to see how much warranty was left on it. They, in turn, referred us to Yukon Tire (love these exotic names) and lickity split we had a replacement. You neglect your tires at your peril in this neck of the woods!

So with that important job taken care of, we began re-packing most of our gear back into all the usual nooks and crannies, while making sure an inventory accompanied the job. Yes, like other rigs, Bridget has been known to eat items now and then! So it's best to know where stuff is being stuffed.

Suzanne is big on lists. She loves order in all facets of her life. While the idea of being able to find things easily appeals to me on a fundamental level, it's obviously not fundamental enough to actually construct an intellectual framework to achieve that goal. So I bumble and fumble along, leaning heavily on her organizational skills to get me through the rough parts.

This reorganization proved tedious. But at least gathering darkness didn't complicate matters further, as Alaska's summer days remain light much longer than in the Lower Forty-Eight states... much, much longer. But while this extra session of light proved a boon, it also provided no cover from swarms of determined, voracious mosquitoes bent on draining every last drop of blood from our bodies. I wish that were hyperbole or at least journalistic license, but it's no exaggeration.

And talk about safety in numbers. The winged marauders attacked in swarm after swarm and in such huge quantities that all but an unfortunate few proved impervious to our increasingly feeble counterattacks. Our flailing and wailing eventually ended in abject surrender, after which we virtually allowed them to have their way with us!

A few pints low on blood, we finally escaped our winged tormentors, leaving Whitehorse for the wide-open spaces, which begin virtually at the city limits. After about five hours of driving through the summer twilight, we found a great free-bie spot overlooking the Stewart River and surrounded by the now ubiquitous tundra-like terrain. And surprise, surprise, guess who was part of the welcoming party? How perceptive of you—a few million more mosquitoes, otherwise known as Alaska's state bird!

The next day proved a perfect case of hurry up and wait. All began well enough. We got off to an early start, wanting to make sure we got to Tok before four p.m. to pick up our mail. It's amazing how letters from home grow in importance the longer you've been on the road without any news of your friends and loved ones.

Unfortunately, most of our mail drops contain more bills, magazines and catalogues than anything else—the written let-ter fast joining the dinosaur in oblivion. Having said that, I should add that any shortage of written letters is more than made up by a daily stream of emails, which are much more immediate.

All went well until we reached Dawson—the former center of the famous Klondike gold fields. Very rustic—very tour-isty—not our cup of tea but still interesting in an artificial sort of way. Anyway, we arrived in Dawson expecting to get right on the ferry across the Yukon River, or, at worst, to experience a short wait.

Talk about a couple of innocents abroad. We could hardly believe our eyes. Without a word of exaggeration, I can tell you there must have been a line of vehicles, mostly RVs, stretch-ing as far as the eye could see. We soon learned why. The lone ferry, you see, takes no more than four vehicles at a time, with priority given to commercial traffic. But no worries. After all, we were on vacation, right?

To help pass the time and relieve the boredom while waiting in line, we took turns visiting the stores, museums and tourist bureaus that caught our eye as we slowly drove by them. I say took turns because one of us had to be in our rig at all times to move her forward as the line inched inexorably towards the waiting Yukon and its lone ferry.

I believe few things happen without a reason. And when they do, one has to employ the lemons-into-lemonade philosophy. So neither one of us was terribly surprised when separate visits to the Northwest Territories Tourist Bureau spawned the same idea of driving the famed Dempster Highway to the territorial capital of Inuvik, not far from the Arctic Ocean.

This had the smell of adventure all over it. And when the territory's deserved reputation for solitude and wide-open spaces was thrown in for good measure, you had the perfect recipe for those of us wanting desperately to escape the madding crowds like those surrounding us at that very moment.

After all, weren't these some of the basic reasons we went small, as in truck camper, rather than purchasing a bigger, more cumbersome, motorhome, fifth wheel or the like? So if that constituted our basic RVing strategy, then the Northwest Territories certainly seemed perfect for us. In fact, its stark, forbidding landscape is about all it has to offer, apart from the fun of meeting friendly inhabitants and the adventure of crossing a couple of rivers on small ferries along the way. And, perhaps most of all, the thrill of crossing the Arctic Circle.

I also had plenty of time to talk to the locals—that is, when I wasn't jumping back into the rig and moving it forward another 10 feet or so. First and foremost, given our circumstances, I wanted to know why no bridge had been built across the mighty Yukon, either here or elsewhere. I must say this was a query based on curiosity, not anger, at our current situation.

The answers I got, while being romantically interesting, were not totally convincing. If I were to believe the locals, the main impediment to building such a bridge wasn't so much the huge amount of ice and snow that accumulates on the river during the long and extremely hard winters. Rather, the real threat to any bridge foundations comes with the onset of spring when mountainous chunks of ice begin to break up, crushing everything in their path as they move downstream.

At least that's the story I got. As I said, I remained somewhat skeptical that I was actually being given the real reason. More likely, this sounded like one specially concocted for inquisitive summer visitors.

For my part, I have to believe that in this age of state-of-the-art-bridge-building technology, any such peril, as formidable as it might be, could be overcome. So maybe it's more a lack of political will or finances, rather than the lack of technological expertise, that ultimately keeps the ferry running. After all, isn't Canada the nation that gave us the monumentally long and complex bridge now connecting the province of Prince Edward Island to the mainland?

I also learned that the exact date of each year's big ice breakup on the Yukon is a highly debated subject during those long winter nights when spring seems so far away. In fact, it could well be part of a highly sophisticated psychological ploy to convince the locals that spring will indeed eventually come, despite the howling Arctic winds and subfreezing temperatures outside.

I was to learn that such predictions have become almost an art form in the region. Now I don't know if hairy caterpillars or the like are examined for clues as to the length and severity of the forthcoming winter. What I do know, though, is that all sorts of "experts" with all sorts of secret theories take part in various "name the exact date and time of the spring ice breakup" contests, raffles and the like, along with almost everyone else in Dawson City and environs. Hey, what better way to wile away those seemingly endless winter days and nights, especially if you're stuck somewhere all on your lonesome?

Hey, I'd like to keep talking to you but, you know what, after four hours of patient waiting, we're next on the ferry. Oops, I might have just jinxed us. On second thought, maybe I should revise that to "I think or I hope we're next on the ferry." After all, we haven't been waved aboard as yet and stranger things have happened. As that great philosopher Yogi Berra once said, "It ain't over 'til it's over." And that most certainly applies to ferry crossings as well!

16

A HAINES WAY OF LIFE

ONE OF the most overused and therefore abused words when it comes to describing the scenery of Alaska, Yukon, Northwest Territories and British Columbia is "spectacular." We writers are all guilty of sprinkling our work with that seemingly all-purpose word, debasing the currency in the process. In fact, I defy you to read any number of travel articles on this part of North America without spotting the dreaded "s" word. When in doubt, it seems, just throw in a "spectacular" and the needed descriptive freight is carried.

But I'm sorely tempted to join my fellow literary lazy-bones in describing the 150 mile drive from Haines Junction, Yukon, to the small American coastal town of Haines with that very same "s" word. In fact, the absolute and constant beauty on view along that entire stretch of road must rank way up there when we tally up this trip's truly memorable scenic experiences.

The centerpiece takes the form of a constant, tantalizing sampling of the outer mountainous fringe of the huge Kluane National Park System, which takes in large portions of British Columbia, Yukon and southeastern Alaska. Eventually this seemingly endless chain of peaks blends seamlessly into the equally spectacular (whoops!) Alaskan-British Columbia Coastal Range.

Mountains of the Kluane National Park on the road
between Haines Junction, Yukon, and Haines, Alaska.

Traveling as one does through four distinct climatic zones, the panoply of beauty on parade is understandably large and varied in the extreme. It's as if you just get through "oohing" and "aahing" over the offerings of one particular zone only to blend into the next with its slightly different but equally entrancing qualities.

And adding to all these many experiences was one final piece of good fortune—bright, sunny, almost sparkling, weather, not to be taken for granted in this part of the world.

Haines itself is rather nondescript at first sight. True, its physical surroundings are highly visually impressive. But the town itself doesn't jump up and grab you by the lapels. Instead, Haines makes you work for your eventual enjoyment as you meet the locals and begin receiving the all important insider tips of what to do and where to go.

Let me put it another way. Haines, like so many other Alaskan towns and cities, needs its daily infusion of tourist dollars and does its best to make sure you leave as many behind during your visit. But one gets the feeling that Haines has a greater substance and background than other municipalities, which seem to exist only to care for the thousands upon thousands of tourists who flood in each summer.

Upon our arrival in Haines we didn't feel set upon; no grasping hands were outstretched in rapacious and phony courtship. We were allowed to explore what the town had to offer on our own terms, with seemingly little concern on the part of the inhabitants as to whether we succeeded or not.

And that was fine with us, because when all is said and done, there's no substitute for exploring. We've all done it. You stumble into a place, making seemingly every possible wrong turn but picking up interesting bits and pieces along the way. This, while driving down little side roads not knowing or caring where they lead, resulted in many great serendipities.

One such unexpected pleasure could only be enjoyed on foot. And soon we found ourselves walking down to a place called Battery Point, which overlooks the lovely Lynn Canal, the pristine body of water that serves as the conduit for the virtual armada of cruise ships carrying their human cargo to Skagway.

About the only land route to Battery Point leads through a large evergreen forest. The well-worn path through this densely wooded area follows the natural contours of the land, crossing streams and using root systems as steps. Standing on the rocky beach that is Battery Point, we were well rewarded with panoramic vistas of the Lynn Canal, surrounded by snow-capped mountains that fall right into the water.

As I contemplated the scene, all the while fighting off the nasty horseflies intent on making a meal of me, three bright-eyed young people emerged from the trail. Come to find out one was attending Bible college in Austin, Texas; the second, just fresh from graduating high school, intended to follow suit; and the third indicated she would most likely do the same, but not for a few years, as she was still quite young. All three seemed to be fired with a missionary zeal and a love of God, which was wonderful to see.

And their mom and dad weren't far away. In fact, their father was the "pistol packin' parson" described in greater detail in another chapter.

Another of Haines' off-the-beaten-track delights is the American Bald Eagle Foundation. Located on the outskirts of the town, the ABEF has long been committed to wildlife education, research and conservation, but not in the bellicose, in-your-face manner of many others working to conserve America's wildlife.

I'm all for the responsible management of our natural environment. I also support folks being able to make a living in order to feed their families. What I'm not in favor of is some folks sitting in their ivory towers, sanctimoniously trying to impose their environmental will on others, with scant regard for or, in some cases, even knowledge of, the economic ramifications of their high-handed, meddlesome, policies.

I was attracted to the ABEF because of its seemingly down-to-earth, realistic approach to the very serious and often controversial job of protecting Alaska's bountiful natural resources. After all, it's only through cooperation between environmentalists and industry that this delicate balance between conservation and economic necessity can be maintained without one side or the other feeling mistreated. And you know that rarely, if ever, does that bring about lasting compromise.

The time to teach this philosophy is when folks are young. When old age fossilizes the thought process about complex conservation issues, changing attitudes becomes a much more difficult proposition.

With this in mind, I applaud the foundation's efforts. While its primary focus clearly lies on the Bald Eagle, it's plain to see this magnificent bird is but one small part of the earth's over-arching ecosystem. And, what's more, the ABEF realizes this complex relationship has to be understood and protected for the mutual benefit of all species, endangered or otherwise.

As noted earlier, first impressions can indeed be seriously flawed. And the more we poked around Haines the more we saw the error of our initial impressions. We had arrived half expecting just another touristy type of Alaskan town, rather superficial and frothy. What we actually got was something more full-blooded and grounded in its history.

So when we finally retraced our steps back the 150 miles to Haines Junction, we left with a greater appreciation of the nature of Haines, coupled with a firm desire to return and scout out more of the town's secret offerings—ones not necessarily splashed across the all-pervasive and persuasive tourist literature.

So if "spectacular" is one of the most overused words in the travel writer's lexicon, another right up there vying for supremacy is "special." It's for that reason that I try very hard to avoid using the word. But when it comes to describing Haines and its inhabitants, the word "superlative" is the one that most readily springs to mind. And it's for that reason that we have it on our "must see again" list for Alaska.

17

THE PISTOL PACKIN' PARSON

DRIVING THE 150 miles from Haines Junction, Yukon, to the small Alaskan coastal town of Haines, we pretty much knew what to expect at the end of the road. We'd checked out all the guidebooks, we'd asked for and received all the big and little tidbits on what to do and what not to do from fellow RVers who'd made the trek before us. And, upon arrival, we'd make a beeline to the local tourist bureau for my usual stack of pamphlets, brochures, booklets and goodness knows what else being given away.

I don't know about you but I'm a hoarder of such stuff. I love collecting all this literature and then sifting through it for all those quirky little out-of-the-way facts. For instance, here's a little gem, courtesy of a small column in one of Haines' finest publications. Did you realize, or even care to know for that matter, that Haines is only 13 miles by water from Skagway but 359 miles by road?

See, that's the kind of esoteric, earth-shattering information that you just don't get everywhere. But it comes with a hefty price tag. Every month or so I have to go through Bridget with a heavy heart and hefty plastic bags giving the heave ho to literally mounds and mounds of these publications that threaten to engulf our tiny living quarters.

Strange as it might seem, these little paper critters appear to take on a life of their own, taking up residence under seats, tables, on counters, beds and every other conceivable flat space. Another reason they appeal to me is that most contain offers for some sort of discount on something or other.

You've seen them. Ten per cent off on your third scuba diving tank, 15 dollars off your second bungee jump or such-and-such a discount on a glacier climbing expedition. I don't know about you, but at my age and physical condition, these aren't exactly at the top of my "must do or buy" lists.

But even though you're 99% sure you'll never use or take up their most generous offers, your frugal instincts just somehow won't allow you to toss them, right? One, two, three. Repeat after me: "Guilty as charged but with extenuating circumstances."

In many respects, I wish I had my wife's attitude towards this literature for tourists and the stupendous offers contained therein. She rarely, if ever, reads any of it, relying instead on her two-legged encyclopedia who seconds as her chief driver and sleeping companion. And believe you me, he'd better have the answer at his fingertips to each and every one of her questions, be it historical, cultural or social, or he'll get an earful, good and proper. I see you men nodding your heads in agreement, so you know exactly what I'm talking about.

With any good fortune, upon reaching Haines we'd see flocks (if that's the correct terminology) of bald eagles literally doing their best pigeon impersonation in terms of sheer numbers and boldness. We knew we'd probably see one or two huge cruise ships heading to Skagway, but bypassing Haines, via the Lynn Canal. And, as usual, we'd see a typical small town (in this case about 2,500 residents) cramped between a sparkling body of deep clean water and seemingly ubiquitous snow-capped mountains.

And, in fact, it was turning out to be just that—one of those memorable but generally predictable trips of accumulated sensory overload. Then, out of the blue, the unexpected jumped up and smacked us, proving yet again that it's generally the unplanned and serendipitous that end up in the category of memorable.

Haines is the kind of town that doesn't open itself up without some effort on your part. In fact, I don't think it would be too unkind to describe the town as being rather nondescript at first blush.

This is not to suggest that there's nothing in Haines for tourists to sink their teeth into, both literally and figuratively. What Haines does is make you earn your eventual enjoyment by way of meeting the locals and gleaning from them those all-important insider tips on what to do and where to do it. Too bad, in this particular case, those tips failed to include how to do it!

As is the nature of things in the Northwoods, towns and cities tend to end rather abruptly, to be replaced by dense stands of evergreens. Trails run through these woods. And it was on one such trail that we found ourselves heading for a stretch of rocky beach called Battery Point, which provides panoramic views of the Lynn Canal.

The path followed the natural contours of the land, crossing streams and pitching ever downwards towards the water. To aid in this process, root systems of the tightly packed evergreens were used as steps, easing the footing from one point to the next.

We were moving deeper and deeper into this heavily forested area when suddenly around a bend in this makeshift path appeared the chap I will forever refer to as "the pistol packin' parson." With him were his wife and three of what we were to learn were his eight children.

True to his moniker, the good reverend was indeed sporting a bright, shiny 44 magnum pistol, which was prominently resting in a holster slung directly under his left armpit. After exchanging effusive greetings, which we had earlier learned was standard among the preponderance of hikers in Alaska, it soon became readily obvious that he was surprised and somewhat perplexed to note that we were out there walking around the woods without, as he put it, "protection."

Being a city boy, the word "protection" immediately conjured up thoughts of a totally different nature. But I immediately realized that was a tangent not relevant in this context, especially when it was a pastor doing the asking.

So preferring to take the high road, I resorted to naivete, blandly asking, "Protection against what?" Well, we've all been in similar situations, right? The minute something really dumb leaves your mouth you know that you've well and truly put your foot in it—and big time. This was one of those moments.

Actually, as we were first beginning our walk, there'd been a rather large and quite prominent sign stating in no uncertain language that bears had been sighted in the area recently. I don't recall whether they'd been identified by exact species of bear spotted. But, to my mind, that detail would be of rather minor consequence if you had one of these critters hot on your trail with nothing but hostile intentions.

But the notice gave us an out by not having a date on it. As highly improbable as that might sound, that's my story and I'm sticking to it! And, as we all know, maulings always happen to other folks, right?

All that not withstanding, let the record show that we had chosen to ignore a clear warning before setting out for some long overdue exercise in totally unfamiliar territory. I know hindsight is always twenty twenty, as the cliché goes. But, upon reflection, I'm forced to conclude that our decision was a dumb idea, with a capital D.

But somewhere in the deep dark recesses of my mind my inner guardian must have been saying something akin to, "Hey Stupid, you've done some crazy things in your life but this takes the cake." Why do I say that? Well, being the big brave, chivalrous, woodsman I am, I naturally let Suzanne go on a few steps ahead, probably thinking that if there were a bear attack she'd at least be able to sound the alarm.

Just kidding. Please, no hate mail denouncing me as a cruel, heartless and totally self-absorbed, not to mention, sexist pig. After all, self-preservation is the strongest of all instincts.

After regaling us with several horror stories about bear maulings, (Oh, thanks loads, Parson, just the trailside tales needed at that point), the good Reverend 44 Magnum then casually asked what we were packing. Totally flummoxed, we were at a loss to even begin understanding what he meant. To our mind, you packed a lunch or a picnic hamper for such a walk but nothing else.

Sensing our confusion, he clarified himself. "What caliber weapon are you carrying on you?" he asked. To which came our reply, "We're not."

More quizzical looks, followed by what I can only describe as total disbelief. "You're tramping around posted bear country with no gun?" he repeated. At that point, with the total stupidity of our situation rapidly sinking in, all we could muster up was a rather pathetic, "That's right."

He persisted: "Surely you have some 'bear spray' on you, right?" What's bear spray, we asked? Whipping out a can of the stuff, he explained that the particular kind he recommended contained cayenne pepper and other ingredients that, he said, bears found highly objectionable.

More to cover our embarrassment rather than any attempt at being a wise guy, I asked him how many bears he had surveyed before reaching this conclusion. We all got a good laugh out of that smart aleck remark, although on hindsight, I must admit theirs did sound a wee bit hollow.

Undaunted, he cited statistics showing that, on average, each year two or three Alaskans lose their lives to bear attacks. But rather than condemning bears as being some sort of predatory man killers, the pastor and all the others I've talked to on this subject before and since have, to a person, jumped to the defense of the bears. To them, the evidence overwhelmingly points to extenuating circumstances provoking the attacks, such as stupid flatlanders strolling through the woods without protection. Ouch, talk about being too close for comfort!

Returning to our situation, Pastor Magnum then outlined the very least we should be doing when hiking through Alaskan woods. And this proved to be very simple advice indeed.

His recommendation: make as much noise as possible. That's right. Contrary to popular belief, one of the most effective ways of avoiding bear attacks is to let them know you're getting near them so you don't catch them off guard.

To the pastor's way of thinking, the surest recipe for disaster is to inadvertently get between a sow and her cub—a big "no no" if you want to stay healthy. So his recommendation was to wear so-called bear bells on your clothing and to make a considerable amount of other noise as you move through the forest.

The general advice is that bears really don't want much to do with us rather smelly humans and will most happily leave us alone if we do likewise. But if they sense that we're trying to mess with their young 'uns, then woe betide us, big time.

Our pistol packin' parson also revealed that he never went

into any woods, no matter how small, without either his pistol or rifle. And he said this is standard practice, not only among the good folks of Haines, but in most other Alaskan towns as well. As he said: "Putting on your gun-bearing holster is as essential as putting on hiking boots and bells, at least when walking in Alaskan woods."

So all this just goes to show you. Sometimes you can learn more about Alaska way out in the deep woods from perfect strangers like our newfound friend, the Pistol Packin' Parson, than you ever can from stacks of tourist literature.

My only regret is that I didn't take the good parson up on his offer to give me a better look at his magnum. He was ready to draw it from its holster and to give me a good feel of its heft, as he put it, but, for whatever reason, I declined his kind offer.

But upon reflection, that proffered experience, coupled with his tutorial on the magnum 44's stopping power and its reputation of being the weapon of choice for protection against bears, might have added that little exclamation point to our remarkable, and totally unforgettable, seminar "Bear Protection and Avoidance 101," conducted trailside in the woods of Haines, Alaska.

18

A TREASURED
TRADITION

THE SHELTERED Harbor B&B in Haines, run by the Ruttingers, Byron, Laura and daughter Mary, was proving to be a real gem, even though we'd picked it out of the blue. Talk about lucking out!

And at this point we needed all the luck we could muster. Only days earlier a devastating and extensive electrical fire had roared through our truck camper as we traveled in a remote area of northern British Columbia. And it was this fire that had forced us to resort to leaving the camper behind for repairs and using the truck part of our rig to travel to Haines. Hence our need for more conventional lodgings there while the good folks at Fireweed RV in Whitehorse, Yukon, were busy making all the necessary repairs to the camper.

What a hardy and resourceful family the Ruttingers were—and ultra friendly to boot. It's a winning combination, especially for anyone having the good fortune to be staying at their lodgings.

In addition to running an excellent establishment, affording spectacular panoramic views of Portage Cove and beyond, the Ruttingers reveled in sharing with interested guests their voluminous knowledge about Haines, in particular, and Alaska in general. And interested we most surely were.

To make matters even better, we were fortunate enough to be there the very day Byron and Mary had returned from subsistence fishing for Sockeye salmon, which were just beginning their annual run up the Lynn Canal and the adjoining rivers and lakes. What's more, they had had a good day, bringing home 26 sockeye caught in their gill nets.

We caught up with the Ruttingers in the throes of preparing the sockeye for either smoking or vacuum freezing to last through Haines' rather mild but nonetheless long, dreary winters. And what an elaborate operation it was.

We got to watch the smoking operation. It was fascinating to see how the sockeye's lovely red flesh was filleted, washed in vinegar, cut into strips and then marinated in a secret Ruttinger family recipe of brown sugar, salt, etc.

Byron approached me almost conspiratorially and, nearly whispering, informed us that the magic was in the "etc!" And no amount of begging or bribery on my part would make them part with the secret they claim was brought to the United States by their forebears who had arrived in Pennsylvania with William Penn. Sounds good to me! After all, such a treasured secret passed down through countless generations of Ruttingers could hardly be expected to be divulged to any Tom, Dick, or Barry, for that matter.

The side yard of their B&B was the venue for this annual family ritual. To be precise, most of the action centered around the bed of their rather ancient and beat up truck, which sat parked adjacent to the Ruttinger traditional smoke house—a surprisingly small grey wooden structure with two holes poked in the sides. Again, we were not permitted to know the exact proportion, names or mixture of the different woods Byron chopped into various kindling sizes to gain, as he put it, just the correct smoking temperature and aroma.

But Byron was willing to give us the rather detailed reasoning behind what he described as being at the heart of the flavor, along with that "secret" recipe, of course. It seems each species of tree not only gives off a different aroma and taste when slowly burned, but each burns at a different rate and temperature level. So the trick is knowing what exact combination of the various woods to use to achieve the desired taste.

Byron said that unlike the specific fish-smoking recipe of more than 350 years standing, no Ruttinger wood-burning formula had been passed down with it. And for good reason. Even if such a formula had been carefully preserved from one generation to the next, it would have eventually become obsolete as the Ruttingers migrated further afield from their original homeland in Pennsylvania. That makes good sense, because the woods of Pennsylvania could hardly be expected to contain the same kinds of trees found in the Alaskan Panhandle or elsewhere, for that matter.

But Byron, Laura and Mary all agreed that this unknown factor was a major part of the challenge, frustratingly quixotic as it might prove year in and year out. They said that invariably just when they thought they had it down to a science, something totally unpredictable would change the entire formula. And that unknown could be as simple, or complicated, as the severity of the previous winter or another of Mother Nature's little jokes!

Ultimately, the proof of the pudding was in the eating, as my dear momma used to say. Hence the first sampling of each year's finished product was a time of great celebration and anticipation. But it was also accompanied by more than a smidgen of tension, realizing that the time for changing anything had long since passed.

The Ruttingers assured us that the ability to discern these yearly differences in flavor nuances was comparable to the discerning palates of wine connoisseurs. And in an effort to prove that very point, the Ruttingers began thrusting samples of various past "sockeye vintages" under our noses, accompanied by challenges such as, "See how different this one tastes!"

My honest opinion? Speaking purely for myself, I'm convinced that I need lots more training as a sockeye connoisseur and for a very lengthy period of time, as I'm a very slow learner. After all, I recognize that this is a very exacting science and not one that can be mastered in a few short years. So bring on the smoked salmon and let the training begin!

To this end, I offered Byron and his family my services as their exclusive taste tester. To sweeten the deal, I even offered to fly up to Haines each year to carry out my assignment! How's that for generosity?

They said they'd sleep on my offer. Come to think of it that's been a mighty long snooze!

It should be made clear that the Ruttingers' initial catch of 26 sockeyes was part of the 50 they are allowed to catch each season under subsistence rights. A strict government regulation stipulates that none can be sold or bartered. They also served us some shrimp, caught under the same conditions, and they, too, tasted fabulous.

Byron looks and sounds like Jesse Ventura, the former professional wrestler who turned the American political establishment on its collective ear by winning a term as Minnesota governor on the Reform Party ticket. A no-punches-pulled type of man, Byron seemed perfectly suited for the equally no-nonsense type of lifestyle exacted by Alaska.

Like others we've met on this trip, Byron and Laura epitomize the modern day Alaskan pioneers, willing to give up the safe, more conventional lifestyle (in this case, Pennsylvania) for one not nearly as mundane and predictable. But this comes as no surprise after you get to know Byron.

Not surprisingly, he champions free enterprise, self-reliance and a true balance between environmental concerns and the ability of families to sustain themselves using Alaska's abundant but fragile natural resources. He told me that he's against limiting access to Alaska's natural wonders to the young and physically fit. Byron said, "How about the others who also want to see this beauty but can only do so by cruise liner or RV? They should not be penalized. To do so is discrimination." Amen to that, even though I'd never heard of any moves, official or otherwise, to limit the numbers of RVers heading north each spring and summer.

Some renegade members of the cruise line industry create their own public relations nightmare by illegally dumping effluent into Alaskan waters. And the resulting heavy state and federal fines following much adverse publicity certainly make the industry no new friends.

Byron also had specific ideas aimed at bridging the two sides in the environmental dispute. Too long and detailed for this telling, they sounded reasonable to me, but then again I'm a cheechako (tenderfoot) of the first order.

But as challenging and seemingly insoluble as these problems appear, Byron allowed that there's no other place on earth he'd rather live than Haines. And by their quiet nods and smiles, wife Laura and daughter Mary agreed wholeheartedly.

19

THE ALL TOO FAMILIAR

THE WAR of words was raging fiercely in Haines. But it wasn't as if this verbal battle was confined solely to this bucolic piece of acreage on the northern reaches of the Alaskan Panhandle. In fact, the scenario is all too familiar throughout Alaska and, for that matter, in many other parts of the United States as well. It pits the various groups of environmentalists against local merchants, commercial fishermen, loggers, etc.

There seems to be general agreement on the fundamental need to protect all of Alaska's natural treasures. That's the good news. It's how best to reach this goal that divides good folks on both sides of the contentious issue.

As far as Haines is concerned, the genesis of this simmering, none-too-friendly confrontation was the severe environmental damage resulting from the illegal dumping of raw sewage and other effluents in its harbor, Portage Cove, by a visiting cruise ship—not once, but twice. Both times the offending company was fined by the state of Alaska, the second time in excess of 1,000,000 dollars.

The number of weekly visits by cruise ships dropped from eight to one in Haines, while in nearby Skagway they jumped to 27. As a result, Haines suffered economically, with some merchants claiming drops in sales of 80% or more. In fact, one or two merchants confided privately that the situation must be rectified or they'd be forced to close their doors.

Adding to the overall economic downturn was word that 20% fewer RVs were heading north to Alaska that summer because of higher fuel prices. But help might be on the way. I heard unofficially that negotiations were underway with some of the more responsible cruise lines to have additional ships stop in Haines rather than sailing right by on their way to Skagway.

The general consensus seemed to be that between six and eight a week would be optimum. That way both sides to this simmering conflict might be somewhat appeased. After all, said one resident, it was hardly worth it for the city to build a dock extension costing more than 2,000,000 dollars for a mere one ship a week.

So it was hardly surprising that many locals felt that the town's substantial budget shortfall would be better solved through increased passenger trade rather than more onerous means. It's not as if Haines is without other means of attracting tourists.

There are two excellent state parks on opposite ends of town. The Chilkat, which means "small fish," affords additional spectacular views of the surrounding mountains and waters, with two extra treats in the form of the Rainbow and Davidson glaciers. The latter dangles halfway off the mountains, pouring icy water into Lynn Canal by way of a lovely waterfall. The Rainbow Glacier slides down the length of the mountain almost caressing Lynn Canal in the process.

The Chilkat's vegetation is lush and full—a perfect place for lurking mosquitoes and horse flies, which attacked us in droves each time we had the temerity to venture forth for photos. But we're told that the horse fly season only lasts a few weeks. Then they mysteriously disappear without a tear being shed by the previously tormented.

With a camera or a video cam, the art and technology of capturing images has certainly come a long way. But I firmly believe that nothing will ever replace what the human eye can comprehend. To my mind, nothing beats being there in person and seeing it for yourself.

Another interesting Haines landmark is the American Bald Eagle Foundation. Inside the foundation's headquarters lies a treasure trove of exhibits that together form a microcosm of life in the Chilkat Valley. They range from the tiny mink to a mighty 1700-pound moose with a rack of antlers weighing 70 to 80 pounds. In fact, there are examples of the Chilkat Valley's more than 100 species of wildlife and fish. And they're all located in one huge room.

But all good things must end—at least for this visit. So around 8 p.m. it was time to grab a couple of take-away sandwiches from Grizzly Greg's and drive the 150 miles of glorious scenery to Haines Junction in neighboring Yukon. Right now, you're probably scratching your head wondering why the heck would we be beginning a nearly five-hour trip so late. But, as we had learned just a few weeks earlier, in this part of the world and at this time of year it never really gets dark dark, just a sort of gloaming that settles in around midnight or later.

So one of our lasting memories will be of sitting in our truck around midnight watching the lovely coastal mountains while eating two of Grizzly Greg's finest.

The reward—an excellent extended view of a grizzly sow and her one-year-old cub contentedly grazing on tender grass shoots right by the side of the road. As is generally the case, we were alerted to their presence by two other vehicles already parked by the side of the road. With mounting anticipation we did likewise and there were the two bears, just going on about their business as if we all didn't even exist.

Not that I'm anything approaching a bear expert, but it seemed to me that Mama was not the least bit concerned by our presence as she made no attempt to stay close to her cub. For its part, baby bear basically did its own thing, while Mama satisfied her appetite several yards away.

There was no doubt that they were grizzlies, what with the distinctive coloration and hump. One by one the bears' visitors left until we were alone with them. Then for some reason I sensed growing apprehension on Mama's part as she purposely began positioning herself between her cub and us. Noting this, we too bid them a fond adieu, not wanting to cause them any further stress. As we drove away we saw that Mama and offspring immediately crossed the highway, something they were not able to do with our truck in the way.

Haines is a real town and not just a tourist trap like Skagway. To be sure, the town merchants will gladly take your money. But one doesn't get the sense that they exist for tourism alone.

The controversy over the number of cruise liners to be allowed into port each week clearly indicates that this industry forms a vital part of the local economy. But most responsible citizens realize that there must be a balance between what the environmentalists feel is best for Haines and unrestricted, unregulated and unfettered pillaging of the finite amount of local natural resources.

Dave Olerud of the American Bald Eagle Foundation said it best: "We must learn to live in harmony with our natural world, using it wisely to our advantage, while being ever aware that we abuse its bounty at our own peril as well." Somehow I feel the good folks of Haines will be able to strike this vital balance. If they fail we will all be the poorer as a result.

20

SKAGWAY AND DYEA– THE TALE OF TWO TOWNS

UNLIKE THE famous Stampeders of 1898, our decision to visit Skagway, Alaska, had nothing to do with gold, although we most certainly wouldn't have knocked back any free samples given out along the way! No putting our lives on the line battling bitter cold, inhospitable terrain and the barest of creature comforts in a wild scramble to reach just the jumping off point for Dawson and the famous Klondike goldfields.

Instead, we simply climbed into our ultra-comfortable air-conditioned truck, Bridget, in Yukon's capital city of Whitehorse, turned south on the Alaska Highway until hitting Klondike Highway Two, and voila, a mere 93 miles further south, there we were in Skagway.

While we didn't have to share the town with thousands of gold-crazed prospectors, we did have to contend with hundreds, if not thousands, of equally maniacal international visitors, these spilling out of several huge cruise liners that just happened to have docked minutes before our arrival. To this day, I'm still not sure what would have been worse.

Imagine the scene. Here we are minding our own business when suddenly we're engulfed by folks literally lying down on the road to have their photos taken side by side, with others kissing that very same pavement.

At the same time, fellow passengers were jostling to have shots taken of them in front of any building. It didn't seem to matter which one as long as it looked old and somewhat gold rushed! And all this frenetic activity on or around the main street of a town designed to accommodate about 800 inhabitants.

I must confess that we've given this outburst of bizarre behavior much thought without being able to quite figure out the motivation involved. If these passengers represented the previous gold-crazed arrivals in the late 1890s, fair enough. Just being alive at that point must have been cause enough for intense celebration.

But for the life of me I'm still trying to figure out what the heck was motivating these latter day intrepid travelers to carry on that way. Maybe the gourmet cuisine on board the cruise liners was not quite up to standard. Or maybe the beauty shops on board had run out of bluing solution! Or maybe someone had tampered with the water supply! The mind boggles.

Scurrying for cover to escape the throngs, we did find some limited refuge in Skagway's historic district. One of the more interesting buildings housed the US National Park Service, officially known as the Klondike Gold Rush National Historical Park.

I won't try to tell you that we were given our own personal guided tour of the extensive exhibits because even away from the outside maelstrom we represented but two additional faces in a sea of other tourists. But to our relief we did find that the Park Service had done a nice job of strictly limiting the number of folks attending each excellent slide presentation depicting the crazy gold fever that engulfed the town between 1896 and 1898. It's hard to believe but during those three short years Skagway saw its population skyrocket to more than 10,000, only to return to near ghost town status by the turn of the twentieth century.

A movie on this remarkable three-year span, with narration by actor Hal Holbrooke, was also well worth 30 minutes, as were the many other exhibits and displays showing Skagway at its most wild and woolly.

But as far as we were concerned, the rest of Skagway was best left to the good folks on the cruise liners let loose on the town for a few short hours to whoop it up and to spend their money. And from what we could tell they seemed most anxious to oblige, buying everything that wasn't nailed down.

Yes, the rest of the historic district offered some appeal, as did some of the side streets, which, by and large, still remained the quiet domain of Skagway's year-round residents. It was here, rather than amidst the hurly-burly of the rather plastic world of Main Street, where the more interesting bits and pieces of life in this town could be found.

If you look hard enough there's invariably the story behind the story. And Skagway proved no exception. So as soon as possible we revved up Bridget and hightailed it out of town in search of the "other" story, otherwise known as Dyea.

Although not well known any more, in its heyday, in those first wild and crazy days of the gold rush, Dyea rivaled Skagway in size and importance. In 1897, not only was the town plotted but it quickly boasted a population estimated at between 5,000 and 8,000.

At that time, the fledging town of Dyea also sported 39 taverns, 47 restaurants, 2 breweries, 7 doctors, 5 bankers and 2 cemetaries. In addition, Dyea had 11 attorneys, which, come to think of it, might go a long way to explaining its current state of affairs!

In fact, Dyea was the jumping off point for the more famous Chilkoot Trail. But the town died a quick death after it was determined that Skagway, with its deep harbor, would form the southern terminus for the Yukon and White Pass Railroad.

The 20 mile round trip to Dyea was magnificent. The gravel road clings to the side of mountains and around every bend scenic vistas abound. We were even treated to an eagle perching rather clumsily in the top of a tall evergreen. It looked like it was drying off its wings—an observation given credence as it coincided with the news that the King salmon were beginning the year's annual run in the Skagway area.

If Dyea was once a serious rival of Skagway for economic supremacy, it's not even a ghost town now. And to note that there's not much to see in Dyea would be a major understatement. In fact, all we saw with our admittedly unpracticed eyes was a couple of building skeletons.

We did notice lots of construction activity around the very beginning of the Chilkoot Trail. We later found out that during the three months of summer about 3,000 folks each year hike the trail between Dyea and Bennett Lake. And, get this, some crazies even now attempt the climb in winter, just to get a "better" feel for the terrible ordeal the stampeders willingly put themselves through while fired up by the lure of gold.

But I doubt these modern day re-enactors want to truly recreate the feat down to its most accurate and burdensome detail. You see, the Canadian authorities required, as an extra precaution, that each stampeder carry hundreds of pounds of food and equipment to help lessen the number of fatalities.

Returning to Whitehorse, we couldn't help but conclude that in many ways Dyea, even in its present-day nothingness, had left a far more indelible and favorable impression on us than had Skagway, with all its tourist trappings. True, Skagway could boast of being the modern-day symbolic hub of depictions of the gritty and raucous life dominating those tumultuous gold rush years, with the US Park Service playing the lead role. But for a more realistic picture of the harsh conditions faced by the thousands upon thousands of stampeders who passed along the Chilkoot Trail, it was Dyea that spoke to us.

Possibly it was the undisturbed atmosphere of the ghost town today. Possibly it was the feeling engendered by looking at the wooden grave markers of victims of an avalanche that swept them to their deaths in April, 1898. Then again, possibly it was our ability to just wander around at our leisure—unrestrained, alone with our thoughts.

And no doubt lurking there in our subconscious and adding to the enjoyment is the fact that on most days Dyea's ability to speak to its limited number of visitors won't be drowned out by the noise and confusion created by thousands of crazed tourists recently let loose from cruise liners.

So the solution is simple: go visit both. Each has something valuable to offer in understanding the lengths to which men will go for gold.

21

A SENSE OF ADVENTURE

As I logged seemingly countless hours behind the wheel of our Ford F-350 diesel truck, I found myself wondering why we were subjecting ourselves, and Bridget, to day after day of tortuous driving through nonstop, drizzling rain, mud, endless potholes and otherwise nasty conditions just to end up at the small town of Inuvik. After all, my perverted Maughan logic kept questioning the sense of taking all this time and trouble to end up in a little place the name of which we couldn't even pronounce properly!

Suzanne and I kept telling ourselves it was to see the outstanding scenery embracing the Dempster Highway (if the sun ever came out long enough for us to glimpse it) and to experience the thrill of crossing the Arctic Circle. We hoped to double our fun by seeing the variety and the sheer numbers of animals not generally found elsewhere, such as the vast herds of Caribou.

While there's no denying the validity of all these reasons, I kept thinking there had to more to it than that—something much more basic, fundamental—even primal, if you will—for us being so willing to subject ourselves and Bridget to this torture.

Notice I didn't use the word "challenge" to describe our experience. Folks too freely talk about the challenge of their Alaskan experience. At the risk of offending them, that's a load of hogwash. I ask you what sort of challenge is there in driving up a well-engineered highway with thousands of fellow travelers in a convoy-like parade? True it's much different than most anything else encountered in the lower forty-eight states, but a challenge it is not.

In a vain attempt to preserve some individuality while searching for an elusive heightened sense of adventure, we decided to drive the Stewart-Cassiar Highway north through British Columbia instead of the more popular and traveled Alaska Highway. But if the truth be known, that, too, failed miserably to live up to its tough reputation. In fact, with every passing mile we found ourselves increasingly asking out loud when the tough bits were arriving, expecting the road to suddenly turn impassable around the very next bend! But the Stewart-Cassiar never bared its teeth, remaining benign right up to where it joined the Alaska Highway, just west of Watson Lake.

So there we were, far from the border with Alaska, still with that unfulfilled feeling of not having yet accomplished anything truly adventuresome and wondering if we ever would during this particular trip. For us, sightseeing without the thrill of adventure is like pie without the ala mode or a hot dog minus the obligatory mustard or ketchup. You get the picture.

There was also the realization that very soon there'll be no truly unique travel experiences left with homogenized tourism mass-produced, with potential problems reduced or even eliminated. But the only problem is that the creation of this virtual cocoon has left the true adventurer with fewer and fewer real adventures and an increased sense of going through the motions.

The vast majority of travelers nowadays want the privilege of talking the talk without having to actually walk the walk. Don't get me wrong. There's nothing intrinsically wrong or dishonest about that. After all, who deliberately puts themselves in harm's way for some silly bragging rights when it can be done easier and safer another way? But for others it's more the journey than the destination itself.

Now before you go labeling us as some sort of elitist snobs thoroughly out of touch with reality, it might be instructive for you to know a little of our background. In 1971, we drove several thousand miles alone from the Ethiopian capital of Addis Ababa to Cape Town, South Africa, in a Volkswagen camper van with our then one-year-old son. Talk about fools venturing in where angels feared to tread! But, having said that, no one can deny it was an adventure of considerable proportions.

So when folks spoke in almost hushed tones about the rough tough driving "challenge" of the Stewart-Cassiar Highway, our frame of reference was our Africa experience and what passed for roads there. And that was a formidable standard, the likes of which we've never come close to duplicating anywhere else.

But one thing is for sure: this in no way, shape or form makes us any better than our fellow travelers to Alaska, Yukon and Northwest Territories. We just have a different frame of reference—no better, no worse, just different.

So it was against this background that we heard about the Dempster Highway, beginning just outside Dawson and stretching hundreds of miles across Canada's tundra-like Northern Territories and ending just short of the Arctic Ocean in the town of Inuvik. Instantly we knew this had the feel of our sort of road—a highway where traveler services were few and far between and where fast-moving weather patterns regularly turn seemingly benign road surfaces into slippery, treacherous, mud baths in the twinkling of an eye.

The long and lonely drive up the Dempster Highway as we
head for the town of Inuvik, Northwest Territories.

You know the old expression about not asking for something
you might well regret. Before we knew it, we were locked in
battle with the Dempster, experiencing first hand what gave
the highway its feared reputation for being the graveyard of
tires, engines and undercarriages.

But it shouldn't have come as a surprise. I remember talk-
ing to a couple of fellow RVers in a campground outside of
Dawson while we were still in the trip's contemplation stage.
And all we heard at that time was a litany of woeful tales of
destruction, all ending with the same simple piece of advice:
DON'T DRIVE THE DEMPSTER!

But what also came through loud and clear was a clear indication that these and others experiencing major problems on
the Dempster had not done their homework. By that I mean
their rigs were very old, bordering on the decrepit, and had
been poorly maintained. What's more, when they displayed

the tires supposedly eaten up by the Dempster, it was clear these were way past their prime, amounting to little more than accidents just waiting to happen.

The Dempster is not a cakewalk. But neither is it a terror if treated with caution and respect, coupled with detailed planning and proper, well maintained equipment. The reality lies somewhere twixt the two, leaving the experienced traveler in no doubt as to the need for caution. As if to emphasize that very point, the Dempster demonstrated that its harsh reputation was not the stuff of exaggerated gossip. It could and would punish the unwary or the foolhardy.

Upon reflection, I'd have to classify the first day as a relative draw, with the highway hitting us with some extended rough spots—the softening up process, if you will. But we were rewarded with beautiful sunny weather, which only made the spectacular views of the Ogilvie Mountain Range on either side of us even more splendid.

As we were to learn very soon, the Dempster was indeed lulling us into a false sense of confidence, giving no hint of the immense driving challenges that lay right ahead. Less than one day later we would be reduced to a virtual crawl by a combination of near blinding rain and wind and resulting icy surfaces. I remember reminding myself over and over again to drive for the conditions, something I'd been told way back when by men who drove for a living.

And as trite as that advice might sound, in most cases that's the key to survival, as one Swiss couple was to find out to their everlasting regret. As we crawled along in what had deteriorated into appalling weather and driving conditions, they flew by us in a rental vehicle going like the proverbial bat out of hell.

They indeed were tempting fate, as, unlike most other highways, the Dempster does not afford the luxury of shoulders.

You're either on the road or off in the boggy tundra. And that's a place to be avoided at all costs.

Unfortunately, we eventually learned that our fellow travelers from Switzerland had indeed careened off the highway, crashing headlong into that unforgiving terrain. They were airlifted by helicopter to hospital in Inuvik, and we were later told that one had died in the accident, while the other had suffered severe paralysis. Score another one for the Dempster, but with obvious extenuating circumstances.

That horrible scenario unfolded on day two between Eagle Plains and the Peel River ferry crossing north of Fort McPherson, a distance of about 150 miles. To say it was a clear victory for the Dempster would be the understatement of the year. If it were a prizefight the referee would have stopped it in the very first round. Let me put it this way: 80 miles in six hours of nonstop driving! Enough said?

But that tells only half the story. As noted earlier, our remaining tale combined more truly sinister weather, of the high winds and torrential rain variety, and a road generously described as a treacherous, muddy, gravel track strewn with potholes, affectionately dubbed "tank traps" by veteran RVers. Once the initial shock passed, it became a mental challenge not to let the road get the better of us and our truck camper.

Another major personal motivation for me was not wanting to have to lie around in black gooey mud changing flat tires. For several miles this meant slowing down to five miles an hour in a sometimes-futile effort to dodge the worst of the potholes, while not slipping off the highly banked road in the attempt.

Lost in all of this was the fact that shortly after leaving Eagle Plains, we crossed the Arctic Circle. We had made elaborate plans to have our photos ceremoniously taken in front of the rather grand sign marking the demarcation. But given the atrocious weather conditions, when we actually got there that thought never entered our minds, especially knowing we'd eventually be passing that exact spot on our way back. So the pleasure could surely wait.

But just when you think that maybe it's simply not worth it, a reward, in the form of a huge black bear running across the tundra right in front of you, makes you reassess your feelings. But, in the final analysis, the greatest reward is the most satisfying sensation that for just a little while you've been able to not only experience the rigors of the wild but also to emerge with one small victory.

Who cares if it's been accomplished while enjoying all the creature comforts within the snug warm cab of your truck. We shouldn't allow reality to intrude into our fantasies, right?

Oh, by the way, we did stop and take the obligatory photos in front of the Arctic Circle marker on our return journey, proving yet again that there's a little bragging rights mentality in all of us! And that includes even those of us who profess to be battle scarred, hard-to-impress adventurers.

22

ARCTIC GREETINGS

WELL... ALMOST. In point of fact, we're actually camped 22 miles south of the Arctic Circle at a little bump in the road called Eagle Plains.

By bump, I mean a rather modern hotel, complete with decent restaurant, lounge, gift shop and showers, plus an adjacent campground and service station, both owned and operated by said hotel. Hey, after a full day's driving on an unpaved road, this place looked like the Ritz Carlton and Hilton all rolled into one!

So far, we really can't complain about the weather over the course of the first 230 miles north on the Dempster Highway. To be sure, we've had lots of rain, sometimes heavy. However, this part of the Yukon is known to get scads and scads of rain. And if you've ever been caught out in a scad of rain without an umbrella, you know exactly what I'm talking about.

Why all this prattling on about precipitation? Well, hold on and I'll tell you. On unsealed roads such as this one, you need only add a drop or two of moisture to get a driving surface concoction not to be messed with. Translation—extremely slippery conditions, not just in spots, but everywhere.

So you can imagine our mood when told that our climatic good fortune was about to come to a screeching halt, with steady rain being forecast for most of the next day. With this in mind we held our collective breath as the second half of the trip on the Dempster promised to get mighty interesting, not to mention slick.

The Dempster Highway starts its run due north 26 miles east of the famed and fabled gold mining center of yesteryear, Dawson. And from where Route Two and the Dempster converge, it's exactly 456 miles from our ultimate destination of Inuvik, capital of the adjoining Northwest Territories.

A panoramic view of Dawson, Yukon, and the
confluence of the Klondike and Yukon Rivers.

That means the Eagle Plains campground puts us almost exactly half way to Inuvik, with only two small ferry crossings and more long stretches of shale-encrusted road still facing us.

If that sounds a wee bit ominous, it's only because it is.

Talk about the horror stories surrounding this potentially deadly combination of extra sharp rocks and tires, especially those the least bit weakened by age or reduced tread. And, believe me, this is not one of those proverbial relationships made in heaven.

We only had to mention the Dempster to evoke wave after wave of horror stories. In fact, we had no sooner begun settling into a campground of the outskirts of Dawson than the seemingly endless tales of woe began.

To hear one chap tell it, this kind of diabolical, ill-tempered and mean-spirited shale was little less than the shale from hell. To his mind, the only thing worse would have been little razor-sharp knives embedded in the road surface designed specifically to rip unsuspecting tires to shreds after just a few miles of driving.

I tend to take such apocalyptic tales with a grain of salt. While reinforcing the need for caution and care in general, living full-time in a home on wheels also teaches one that a lack of preparedness and faulty or badly maintained equipment also play a major role in such "oh, woe is me" tales. For, if the truth be told, in more instances than not, the devil invariably can be found lurking in these details.

And, sure enough, with just a little probing, our doomsayer rather reluctantly allowed that, oh yes, he had indeed tried the Dempster run with old, worn out tires, which were el cheapo non-radials to begin with. Gee whiz. You wonder about folks sometimes. Wouldn't you just love meeting this yahoo as he careens down the road in his rather large motorhome spitting bits of tires in all directions, while cursing the road conditions at the top of his lungs.

It had taken us about eight hours to drive the 230 miles to Eagle Plains. I can't say I necessarily poked along. What I distinctly remember is making several stops right off the bat to admire the stark, totally denuded Ogilvie Mountains, which, like grey sentinels against the cloudy blue skies, rose up to 7,000 feet on both sides of the road.

And speaking of these clouds, let me go out on a limb and say they're like nothing I've ever seen in the Lower Forty-Eight. In many cases, they're strung out as if caught in some upper atmosphere hurricane. And this observation was pretty much verified by none other than a workman on an area road crew.

In fact, if we're stopped for any appreciable time for road construction or repairs, I never miss the opportunity to chat with any crew member who'll stand still for a few seconds! What better and easier way to get good, interesting tidbits of local knowledge from folks. These people, from my experience at least, really enjoy talking to tourists, if for no other reason than to pass the time of day when their job is to stand around anyway.

When not admiring the amazingly spare, almost forbidding, landscape, we were continually keeping a weather eye peeled for beasties said to call this area of Yukon home. Previous visitors had bragged of seeing lots of bears and the occasional moose. But, so far, our visual trophies have been restricted to caribou and then only the way-off-in-the-distance variety.

Until now, the scenery, though mainly barren and stark, has at least contained the occasional tree, though admittedly, fairly stunted. However, as we travel further north we'll reach the no-tree zone, where it's just tundra, tundra and, for variety, more tundra!

As one would imagine, winters around these parts are only for the hardiest of the hardy. You lose me real fast when you start talking about mountainous snow banks, high, bitingly freezing winds with nothing to slow them as they careen southwards from the Arctic, and temperatures reaching as low as a balmy 40 degrees below zero Fahrenheit. Brrrr... just writing about such chilly conditions has me reaching for hot chocolate, my favorite thick woolen sweater and those fleece-lined slippers I love.

And as if to add insult to injury, a local told me there's a place where the Dempster gets pinched between two mountains. There, he says, wind gusts can reach as high as 90 mph as they funnel down through the small gap.

What's more, my informant added, when that happens, nothing, not semi-trailers, not any sort of motorhome, fifth wheel or the like and, most certainly, no mere automobiles have any chance whatsoever of staying on the road. And believe me, when you leave the Dempster, you invariably end up in the boggy tundra, with the distinct possibility of staying put for a long, long time.

We've been warned not to expect too much from Inuvik. But that was fine because our expectations were never all that high in the first place. After all, when even the tourist literature fails to wax poetic about the place, it's hardly a ringing endorsement.

All that marks Inuvik as our sort of town: quiet, down to earth, unpretentious and so out of the way that folks like us really have to make an effort to get there. This, to our way of thinking, tends to limit the gawkers and the "because it's there" crowd.

After spending some time in and around Dawson, we could really take a town like Inuvik to heart. We had originally planned to spend a very short time in this fabled gold mining center of years past, preferring instead to spend our time checking out where and how that precious metal was actually mined.

But before doing that, we were reluctantly forced to spend an extra day in Dawson getting caught up on chores that you can only do in a city, such as banking, grocery shopping (talk about high prices) and mailing correspondence.

Hey, we don't want you to think we have something against the former capital of Yukon per se. What's more, it most certainly was not the folks living there. They were great. It's just that the place has this decidedly artificial look and feel to it.

A rather small example. A very high percentage of the city's business names contained some reference to the city's golden past. It's either Bonanza this or Gold Claim that, to the point of making the place look and feel like something right out of Disney World or Disneyland.

Even though this tends to be one big turnoff for us, we can certainly understand why the city fathers decided to go total tourist. After all, what other options did they have after the decision was made in 1953 to move the territorial capital, lock stock and bureaucrats, so to speak, just over 300 miles south southeast to the thriving city of Whitehorse.

You've heard of the movie "Back To The Future?" Well, long before that film was ever thought of, the movers and shakers of Dawson decided to institute their own version of back to the future. No longer able to depend on the revenues inherent in being the seat of government, Dawson decided to launch a second gold rush, 57 years after the original.

Now, just over 50 years later, the reinvention is complete, with Dawson superficially, at least, now looking and feeling somewhat like it must have near the turn of the 20th century when the gold seekers poured into the area.

Now all we tourists have to do to make the illusion complete is to cooperate by overlooking a few minor details like cell phones, ATMs, bare midriffs and pierced navels, eyebrows, tongues and goodness knows what else. Then, for good measure, try not to notice the long summertime lines of motorhomes, fifth wheels, cars, trucks and assorted other vehicles all slowly snaking their way through the center of town waiting to board the free ferry. Now that's not asking too much, is it?

After failing in our attempt to accept this illusion, we decided it was more than time to get back to more pleasant and less demanding matters such as visiting a restored gold dredge that had operated on Bonanza Creek just outside of town beginning in 1912. What a huge complex operation, which, we were told, turned out to be one of the very few such dredges that actually paid for itself.

For in the 20 odd years it scoured the soil between permafrost and bedrock, our most excellent guide told us this now fully restored dredge extracted gold worth 12,000,000 dollars. And that was when gold sold for about 14 dollars an ounce. So you can just imagine how astronomical that figure would be in today's dollars.

We then took a steep and circuitous drive up to a nearby scenic overlook called The Dome. Talk about a panoramic view—it was just short of 360 degrees. It was indeed magnificent and well worth the drive.

Spread out far below us was Dawson, which, from this vantage point, could no longer hide what it really was—a small town of just over 2,000 inhabitants with no particular beauty or charm, with mostly unpaved streets that quickly surrendered meekly to the surrounding vastness that is the Yukon.

Of far greater interest, to us at least, was our bird's eye view of the confluence of the Klondike and Yukon Rivers. It was fascinating to see how the clear, clean waters of the Klondike are ultimately swallowed up by the more voluminous and much muddier waters of the Yukon—but not until the Klondike's flow of water had cut a significant swath along one side of the Yukon for several hundred feet before losing the battle against insurmountable odds and being swallowed up.

The vast landscape laid out before us also revealed what turned out to be miles and miles of tailings or mounds of dirt

127

and rocks from the many gold dredges, large and small, that operated in and around Dawson for about 60 years. For all intents and purposes, the countryside looked like the playground of some huge, insatiable mole that had spent its entire lifetime tunneling underground for food and depositing the soil debris topside. And almost everywhere this untiring rodent tunneled, it stood a good chance of hitting pay dirt.

It was this very same allure of instant, easy riches that drew tens of thousands of gold-fevered adventurers to this area just before the turn of the 20th century. But while only a comparative few ever struck it rich, they all combined to leave an indelible and fiercely distinctive imprint on this beautiful yet unforgiving land.

And it could be argued that much the same scenario is being played out to this very day, with the land grudgingly giving up its wealth to only the determined and fortunate few. But with one monumental difference. Those stout-hearted men and women of yore were on their own, whereas today's locals can count on at least four good months to fatten their wallets on a continual stream of tourists before hunkering down for another cold, hard northern winter.

23

ELVIS LIVES!

DON'T LAUGH. I know what you're thinking—those long, Arctic summer days (the Land of the Midnight Sun and all that jazz) and the resulting truncated nights of fitful tossing and turning in the gloaming must have finally taken their toll on the old coot. In fact, some might even attribute my Elvis sighting to a hallucination directly resulting from prolonged sleep deprivation.

To be fair, I, too, might have readily subscribed to that theory if I hadn't been 100 percent, no doubt whatsoever, convinced that I had indeed seen Elvis Aaron Presley in the flesh with my own two eyes.

Still not convinced, you say? After all, it must be noted that I do wear fairly strong lenses in my glasses.

Well here's the clincher. Thank goodness I had the good fortune of having an impeccable second eyewitness in my very much down-to-earth, highly logical and solidly grounded wife, Suzanne. She would also swear on a stack of Bibles that together we saw Elvis during our recent visit to Inuvik—a small city in the far reaches of Canada's Northwest Territories, located just a long stone's throw from the Arctic Ocean.

No, he was not busy picking up tickets to some event left

him by adoring fans. And neither had he just left the building! In fact, he was very much inside a building, doing what Elvis does best, meeting and greeting his appreciative public.

I mean to tell you, there he was, large as life (and getting bigger by the day, judging by his girth), signing autographs at Inuvik's local community library for an enthusiastic knot of adoring young fans. And for you remaining doubting Thomases out there, let me ask you one question: how many times have you tried to pull the wool over a youngster's eyes? I can tell you from personal experience that it's impossible. And, as cleverly evasive as you think you've been, the reality is that the little dickens find you out every darned time!

Those little Inuvikians were eating it up. Not only were they part of such a select group of fans actually getting up close and personal, but they were actually getting Elvis's genuine autograph to boot. What could be better?

Hold on there—I know what you're thinking, what with all these untold thousands of Elvis impersonators running around hither and yon ripping off the King. With all that in mind, I have no hesitation in telling you that this had to be Elvis, no doubts whatsoever.

He looked like Elvis right down to the thick sideburns and sunglasses, he dressed like Elvis and he even signed his name Elvis Presley.

So what more proof do you want? After all, he did have that special sequined look. In fact, his clothing could not have been more Elvis-like if he had tried.

He had on the regulation white jump suit complete with the requisite hundreds of sequins and matching white bell-bottomed trousers with a little adornment on them as well, just for good measure. His outfit was perfect, right down to the multicolored eagle on his back and the huge rings of various shapes and colors on his pudgy fingers. Eight rings for eight fingers! In fact, he even bulged in all the right places, showing that life must have continued to be good after he, shall we say, decided to drop out of sight for a spell.

All right, all right, so he was driving an older car, a small 1980-ish compact Arcadian model made by GM of Canada. But before you go jumping to conclusions and trashing him as just another of those phony balonies out there committing fraud, consider this: that little semi-antique was covered from stem to stern with Elvis memorabilia of every conceivable size and description. The back bumper was awash with stickers proclaiming a love and belief in Elvis, as were the side panels and front bumper. In fact, come to think of it, the entire car was festooned with so much Elvis-related stuff it looked like a moving and grooving shrine to the King!

But in the interest of what's left of journalistic integrity, I report that the intervening 20 or so years since it first rolled off the assembly line had not been particularly kind to Elvis's ride. In fact, whether Yukon's cold, cruel winters were the chief culprit or not, the King's wheels were in dire need of a new paint job.

That's being kind. The harsh reality was that a once vibrant and shiny red color had slowly morphed into a decidedly dull, off-orange hue of varying shades, depending on the angle of viewing. And let's face it, all those rust spots weren't going to get any smaller without lots of tender loving care, augmented by liberal dollops of cash.

Now I'm not in any way intimating that the King was temporarily low on funds. Let's put it this way: at that moment he most likely was suffering an embarrassment of cash flow!

But talk about loyalty. The locals, both young and old alike, seemed genuinely perturbed that I should have the audacity to even point out some of these anomalies. They quickly noted that his usual wheels, one of those big old Cadillacs with sporty fins, was undoubtedly in the mechanic's shop undergoing minor repairs.

What's more, and by way of offering further proof of his legitimacy, these very same upstanding Inuvikians told me that Elvis had been knocking 'em dead at the city's liveliest nightspot, The Mad Trapper Pub. And that glowing opinion was shared by paying customers who confirmed that Elvis was, in fact, putting on quite a show.

But I must confess that even I needed a little more convincing, so I did some checking. Now if this isn't the clincher, then I don't know what is. Elvis Aaron Presley is in fact this man's legal name, rather than Gilbert Nelles, the one his mommy and daddy gave him upon his birth way back on July 28, 1956.

That's right, the Canadian High Court has ruled as much. The legal opinion was that no good reason could be found not to grant the application for a legal name change.

Gilbert's decision to become Elvis in both name and spirit came several years earlier, back in 1990, to be exact. The then Gilbert Nelles says there was no holding him back after, he claims, the real Elvis appeared to him. Moments later, he recalls, he saw himself standing in front of thousands of people, singing on stage, wearing a maroon-colored outfit. Gilbert claims the clincher was an energy force coming off him that was so strong he had to shield his eyes from the glare of the stage lights over him.

But what preceded that is even more interesting. Gilbert says he and his girlfriend were visited by an alien object that hovered over his head all the while shining a bright beam of light over him. A short while later, Gilbert says aliens spoke to him, with one apparently entering his body, beginning his transformation to Elvis Aaron Presley.

The rest, as they say, is history. Gilbert says about four or five months later he started singing. At the same time, he dyed his hair black, something he says he would never have thought of doing earlier.

In fact, to further prove his point, Elvis later produced his own mildly successful CD and cassette with a title that proudly proclaims, "Still Living." And to further legitimize his new name, a film documentary, called *The Elvis Project*, chronicles the musician's tour of Yukon in 2001. Supported by a 5,000 dollar government grant, the documentary is truly a grass roots project, with the balance of the funding coming from everyday citizens of Yukon and local businessmen.

In 2004, the documentary debuted in Las Vegas, after being successfully screened at several North American film festivals. In fact, in New York it won an award for Best Experimental Documentary. One critic has praised The Elvis Project for its "refreshing, nonlinear, multimedia storytelling style as it takes the viewer on a road trip with Elvis and his band, The Armageddon Angels, as they play to packed houses in Yukon."

So there. I now officially give you permission, once and for all, to forget about all those other rumors you've heard. You know the ones—those saying Elvis is a bartender in a little town in Arkansas or the ones that place The King down somewhere on Mexico's Baja Peninsula, where he passes as a local fisherman.

Trust me when I tell you this Elvis Aaron Presley is the real deal—the genuine article. And to think we stumbled across the real McCoy Elvis in the most unlikely of places—the tiny city of Inuvik.

But before you rush out to buy those airline tickets to fly north, let me give you an additional piece of invaluable information. My usually reliable informants tell me that Elvis currently makes his home in a little town south of Yukon's capital, Whitehorse.

Now you're on your own. Oh, one last bit of advice. If I were you, while you're hanging around doing your best private eye impersonation in Whitehorse, check out every little red Arcadian that drives by. There can't be that many still on the road after all these years. You most certainly won't be able to mistake the one owned by the King, Elvis Aaron Presley. It is, after all, unique. Just ask yourself this: how many little red Arcadians drag their mufflers on the ground?

Maybe it's been fixed by now, but when we caught up with him on his way out of Inuvik and told him about his slight muffler problem, we received our final proof of his authenticity. After receiving our news, he simply smiled, shook my hand and said in a vintage Presley-accented voice: "Thank you, thank you very much."

Now if that isn't the absolute, lead pipe clincher, I don't know what is!

24

THE END OF THE LINE

THE BEST and most descriptive word to describe Inuvik, the capital of Canada's Northwest Territories, is "fascinating." Quaint has a certain condescending quality to it. Lovely, in the truest sense of the word, it most certainly is not. And the descriptive "garden spot" also falls wide of the mark.

So we're left with "fascinating" or possibly "unique" to describe this town of just over 3,000 that immediately becomes the unofficial Holy Grail of every traveler beginning the long, often demanding, 456 miles of road that is the Dempster Highway.

Inuvik's physical location is very impressive indeed when one considers that it lies 200 miles north of the Arctic Circle and a mere 60 miles south of the Beaufort Sea. And in this regard, the town residents are quite proud of the fact Inuvik was "the first community north of the Arctic Circle built to provide the normal facilities of a Canadian town." And it says so right on the town's official monument.

My first impression as we drove into town was that it was kind of rough around the edges. The weather didn't help either. It had been raining, so the streets, including the main drag, were muddy.

Then something else much more significant caught my eye. All of Inuvik's water, sewer, heating and power sources are elevated above the ground on a network of metal cradles. And the sight of them snaking from one building to another all over town is almost worth the effort of getting there. Yes, on second thought, "unique" is indeed an excellent way of describing Inuvik.

But, having said that, there was something camp about the place. You know the old beatnik definition of camp—something that's so far out of style that it's actually in style. But believe you me, it's not a penchant for style that's the chief motivating force behind the above ground plumbing and other facilities. It's necessity, pure and simple. If convention ruled and the pipes were laid underground, most services would grind to a halt with the onset of Inuvik's winter, which sees temperatures dip to rather the chilly side, to say the least.

Apart from Inuvik's unbelievably long and harsh winters, the other main reason for the above ground piping is permafrost. The whole town, and indeed the entire region, sits on this permafrost, which thaws only slightly during the summer.

In fact, every building in Inuvik sits on special posts driven deep into the permafrost for stability. It's no wonder the locals have great respect for permafrost, which has a deserved reputation of being quite unstable and therefore disturbed at your peril.

After a quick tour of town we found a great restaurant. In fact, it became our regular culinary hangout for our remaining three days in town.

The first night it was musk ox roast, which was quite yummy, not gamey in the least, and tasting a lot like lean beef. The second night we settled on a combination of caribou and Arctic char, which the locals described as a salmonoid-type fish with a rather bland taste. To my palate, the caribou was a little gamier than the musk ox, but Suzanne much preferred it. The third night I had a musk ox burger while Suzanne opted for one made of her favorite, caribou.

Inuvik's Catholic church known affectionately as "The Igloo."

Living up to its reputation of not being a tourist trap, Inuvik almost makes you seek out your enjoyment. It's not just served up on a platter for you. Sure, there are a number of gift shops and boutiques on the main street where you'll be charged an arm and a leg for locally crafted items. But no one is out there hustling customers on the sidewalk.

If you want to buy something, then you have to do all the running. In fact, I got the decided impression that the locals much preferred it this way, with any other way of doing business considered crass and less than professional.

This is not to say there's nothing worth seeing in Inuvik. Case in point: driving around the outskirts of town we spied a rather dilapidated former hockey arena. A closer look showed that it had been converted into a huge indoor garden, glass roof and all, where individuals had plots designed to extend the existing minuscule growing season.

Almost instantly we were engaged in a detailed conversation on the finer arts of gardening with a local woman who insisted on giving us all her precious beans as a gift. She reckoned they'd have to wrap things up by the end of September as it would cost too much to heat the building, even though the heating fuel was from the town's own natural gas well.

The government had recently returned the land to the indigenous people. As a result, the tribal councils were buying up all the viable businesses in Inuvik with revenues from the considerable oil and gas fields located just outside of town.

As one would imagine, the big oil companies were tripping over themselves to get part of the action. And no wonder, given the assessment by one oil executive I spoke to that the known gas reserves in the region were in the trillions of feet. That's known, not estimated. And that same executive told me that the gas was already capped, just waiting for the most economical way to get it to market.

At the time, the biggest debate was over the merits and demerits of two competing marketing strategies. One involved liquefying the gas and shipping it around Alaska and down Canada's west coast to energy-hungry American companies. The other involved the building of a pipeline down across Alberta and into the United States similar in concept to the Trans-Alaska pipeline from Prudhoe Bay in the north to Valdez in the south.

While we were fortunate to just happen upon the converted hockey arena, there's no missing Inuvik's most formidable and impressive building, which stands smack dab in the middle of town on the main road. It's the Catholic church, but in keeping with local traditions, it's in the shape of an igloo. We took a look around inside and while the interior was quite nice, I'd have to say that clearly the church's most compelling feature lies in its unusual exterior shape.

The town has the feel of having seen better days. Despite that, you also had the keen sense that everything could begin busting loose at any moment, what with oil and gas being found right next door and in prodigious amounts to boot. After all, oilmen from around the world were not filling the bars and hotels for the scenery alone. And believe you me, there were plenty of them.

Let's hope that when energy jobs start opening up, first consideration is given to hiring and training the local indigenous population. For the sad fact remains that far too many remain either unemployed or underemployed.

However, we were hearing encouraging assurances in this regard. Far stricter conditions of doing business were being laid down by Inuvik's indigenous leadership as they began flexing their increasing financial and political muscle.

Earlier in our travels, we had a met a young couple in Fairbanks who had nothing good to say about Inuvik—the place or the people. In fact they went as far as to advise us not to bother with it.

I'm so glad we didn't heed that advice. For if we had, we would have missed one of the more interesting stops on our entire tour of the north. Unvarnished and rough-hewn it is, but there's also an authenticity about Inuvik that, to our minds at least, makes getting there well worth the effort.

25

A HIDDEN GEM

I DON'T know if anyone ever intentionally sets out to visit the tiny town of Eagle while planning their tour of Alaska. This is in no way a put-down of the tiny settlement, but merely a fact.

In fact, when we were preparing our assault on the 49th state, the suggestions flying fast and furious from well-meaning friends centered mostly on the usual tourist suspects, such as Fairbanks, Seward, Valdez, Homer and the like. But no one ever approached us and said something like: "Oh, your trip to Alaska won't be complete unless you visit Eagle!"

After all, it's not as if Eagle's on a well-beaten road between two major tourist destinations. You really have to purposely want to visit it. And, as a result, not many visitors get to see this enchanting town of about 150 inhabitants.

Possibly the biggest obstacle to increased tourism is the twisty-turny road that clings to the sides of mountains for a good deal of the nearly 65 miles down to Eagle. And I use the word "down" without fear of contradiction!

If you check your official maps, you'll see that stretch of road goes by the more officious and benign title of the Taylor Highway. But believe me, when you're busy negotiating those hairpin turns, you're calling the road many other names, none of which remotely resemble highway.

If you're telling yourself that you've heard of that road name before, it's probably because the Taylor is the shortest route from the Alaska Highway to Dawson, Yukon. In fact, the Taylor connects with the famous or infamous (depending on your experience!) Top of the World Highway, which takes you the rest of the way to Dawson, ending in a ferry boat ride across the Yukon River.

Another reason why the Taylor might stick in the memory bank is the fact that it takes you to that super metropolis of Chicken. Little more than wide spot in the road, Chicken attracts a staggering number of visitors when one considers what's there or, more to the point, what's not there.

Maybe it's the name. Or maybe, unlike Eagle, Chicken has dressed up what little it does have to turn itself into a certified tourist trap. And if that was the intent of the good fathers of Chicken, then they've succeeded beyond their wildest dreams.

But let's face it, the biggest thing going for Chicken is ease of access. All you have to do is get on the Taylor Highway, drive a certain number of miles on a generally good surface, and voila, you run smack dab into Chicken. No muss, no fuss. And even if you end up being a wee bit cheated at the disparity between hype and reality, it was, after all, an easy ride there. So that takes the sting out of any feeling of disappointment.

Not so the other town also sporting a bird's moniker. After turning at the junction with the Top of the World Highway about 30 miles down the road from Chicken, things begin to get very interesting.

We have a relatively small truck camper, so when we read the Milepost's very detailed description of what lay ahead we didn't dissolve into fits of apoplexy. A word to the wise: never,

I repeat, never venture up to Alaska without the latest edition of the *Milepost*. It is a must.

But if I owned one of those humongous beasts that regularly ply Alaska's main highways, those same words would have struck fear into my soul. In fact, I'd go as far as to say that my ample chrome dome would have been glistening with little beads of sweat at the mere contemplation of the attempt. And it would be safe to say that Eagle would have been instantaneously scrubbed off that day's itinerary in favor of more accessible destinations.

Here's why. The following are but a few of the *Milepost's* warnings to motorists thinking about driving the Taylor Highway to Eagle. "CAUTION: Rough road, slippery when wet." "CAUTION: Steep, narrow, winding road northward... Slow down for hairpin turns." "CAUTION: Watch for small aircraft using road as runway." And these are but a sampling of the warnings given at regular intervals along the entire 64 plus miles between the junction with the Top of the World Highway to the point where the Taylor becomes Amundsen Avenue as it enters Eagle.

So who can blame all but the most adventuresome in smaller rigs from keeping Eagle firmly on their future list of Alaska things to do? But for those of us who take up such challenges, the rewards at the end of what turned out to be a rather mild experience were more than worth the sense of foreboding felt while negotiating every hairpin turn in the road.

It's strange how a mere 64 miles can seem like an eternity when you're expecting to come face-to-face with a potential disaster around every hairpin turn. But, as I said, the Taylor proved very benign, given that we were aided in great measure by accurate directions and by Lady Luck.

Not that I'm overly superstitious (no rabbit's feet hanging from Bridget's rear view mirror), but I do believe in such things as Lady Luck and Murphy's Law! After all, to what else can you attribute the fact that we just happened to pass the very few other vehicles we encountered on the widest possible parts of the road? Methinks that sometimes it's just your lucky day. Don't question it. Just say thanks and keep moving.

We love out-of-the-way, non-touristy, type of places (that's why we full-time in a truck camper) and never thought we'd find one in modern-day Alaska. But, guess what—if there's ever a place that fits that description, it's Eagle.

No screaming banners welcoming you to town or obtrusive advertising signs enticing you to part with your money on this or that souvenir. I guess the best way to describe Eagle is that it's just your regular, run-of-the-mill town. It just happens to be located smack dab in the middle of the Alaskan wilderness on the banks of the Yukon River.

I recall visiting the unpretentious town library and asking for any available tourist literature or any other information on Eagle, for that matter. The material proffered was helpful, but certainly not gaudy or chest thumping.

We were then left to our own devices to find a place to camp, a chore made somewhat more challenging given the fact that Eagle had no organized campgrounds. But that's never been a problem for us because we're fully self-contained. And as we had prepared for this eventuality by emptying the waste water storage tanks in our truck camper ahead of time, we were good to go for a week or so if we were careful.

There's not a lot to see in Eagle, but what they do have to offer is very interesting indeed. On land, the Fort Egbert National Historic Landmark is a must-see. An old US military establishment, it celebrated its centennial in 1999. And those wanting a better historical perspective have only to enter the Granary building, one of five remaining original structures left intact, for an interpretive exhibit and photo display of days gone by.

By way of a little history, Fort Egbert was an important communications center when the Washington-Alaska Military Cable and Telegraph System was completed in mid-1903. But when that system was eventually overtaken by the newer wireless technology, Fort Egbert declined in importance until it was abandoned in 1911.

Eagle maintains its position as an important jumping off point for journeys up and down the Yukon River. When we visited, the Yukon Queen was still making daily round trips between Eagle and Dawson in neighboring Yukon. Down river, the Yukon flows through the Yukon-Charley Rivers National Preserve and on to the town of Circle.

But as is generally the case, just politely poking around and talking to locals can reap memorable benefits and unexpected pleasures. And Eagle proved to be no exception. While looking for a nice out-of-the-way place to park Bridget for the night, I struck up a conversation with Anne, the principal of the tiny but nicely appointed local community school.

As we chatted she made it known that her most important ongoing project was trying to establish a small, low-powered, FM radio station to be operated by the older students. All students in the high school grades were being encouraged to take part but especially members of the local indigenous Han Athabascan people, who make up about half the school's enrollment. An added benefit would be the station's ability to provide Eagle with much needed local news and entertainment, while serving as an important training facility.

Since I'm a professional journalist and broadcaster with more than 30 years of experience, this project immediately piqued my interest. With my limited help after our first meeting, Anne persisted to the point that the radio station has become a reality, despite the many financial and administrative hurdles placed in her path.

And you'd be amazed at the number of those obstacles, not only by the folks in Washington. The Canadian government had serious concerns as well, given the close proximity of Eagle to the Yukon border. But firmly believing in the need to open up the US broadcasting profession to the widest number of peoples, and being totally committed to that belief, Anne has made her dream come true, whereas a lesser person would have given up long ago.

To my mind, Anne epitomizes the type of hardy individuals who carve out lives in such seemingly inaccessible places as Eagle. Let's face it. It's highly unlikely that Eagle will ever return to those halcyon days before the turn of the 20th century when it enjoyed a population of around 1,700. And I dare say the current residents of this tiny town would cringe at the mere thought of any such rebirth, much preferring the current, more laid back, almost sleepy, atmosphere.

I know we would. But then again we don't have an official say in the matter. We're only visitors who were most appreciative of everything and everyone Eagle had to offer in the here and now. And with this in mind, we can only hope that Eagle will be same when we again visit in the very near future.

26

DOUBLE OOPS!

IT'S NOT as if I woke up today and decided out of the clear blue sky to screw up, not just once, mind you, but twice. I can hear myself now: " Well, Barry, time for you to make a complete fool of yourself again 'cause you're way overdue! And while you're at it, why not make two whoppers today for good measure. That way it'll be twice as much fun!" Not a chance, and don't even try to convince me otherwise!

The day began innocently enough with some extra sleep and a shower in a nice little campground in Glenallen, Alaska. In just a short while, we'd be heading down the Richardson Highway, bound for the pipeline terminus town of Valdez, just over 120 miles away.

But work before pleasure and, try as I might, there was just no ignoring that there was still one "little" chore left to finish before heeding Willie Nelson's advice to get back "on the road again."

Among RVers that job is euphemistically called dumping. I won't go as far as to say it sends chills running up and down their spines. But it comes close. Put another way, it's just a tiny step above having a root canal done!

Suzanne posing under a section of the Trans-Alaska Pipeline.

At best, it's a necessary evil. At worst, it's the job from hell. But no matter how much you curse it out, dumping still has to be done regularly, unless, that is, you're fortunate enough to have that first-ever RV that dumps itself automatically, without anyone's help! Fat chance!

If you're an experienced RVer (no matter the size, make or model of your rig) dumping is something you've done, albeit reluctantly, hundreds of times without major incident. That's because unlike most jobs around your RV, you realize there's simply no room for error. Aah, there's nothing like stark, raw terror to keep one's mind focused like a laser beam!

Having said all that, this particular morning something went terribly wrong—in fact gallon upon yucky gallon of terribly wrong! Bear with me as I try to make this as antiseptically clear as possible. As I loosened the main sewer attachment under the camper, in preparation for connecting the actual sewer line to the dump station, gallons upon gallons of vile-smelling black water poured all over me and then on to the ground, quickly creating a reeking quagmire of monumental proportions. Best left unsaid what I smelled like!

After what seemed an eternity, rather than the mere seconds it actually took, I finally re-seated the sewer attachment but not before being bathed in this foul stew from head to foot. Confused and embarrassed, I mentally scratched my head as I tried to figure out what the heck could have possibly gone wrong. After all, hadn't I always been so carefully precise when it came to this less-than-charming operation?

An explanation was not long in coming. A subsequent examination of the inside opening and closing bayonet mechanisms for both the gray and black water lines revealed the problem, which was traceable back to our last campground stay in Anchorage. There we had been connected directly to the sewer and I had simply forgotten to re-close the valves after unhooking. It was yet more reinforcement for what Suzanne always tells me: "There's always a logical explanation for everything!" But, then again, I've rarely been accused of being logical!

But even though I had solved the riddle of the gushing wastewater, my problems were by no means over. Far from it, in fact. There was still the minor matter of Lake Stinkwater to contend with—a problem only getting worse by the minute given the rising temperatures.

As much as I longed to be rid of my putrid smelling clothes, my main concern right then was cleaning up my mess before anyone else noticed, thus avoiding a big-time embarrassment. To lessen my sense of guilt and shame, I tried to rationalize, to little avail, that it's a case of reluctant familiarity for most fellow RVers. In fact, it's said that you haven't truly been initiated into the RVing fraternity unless something equally or even more catastrophic has befallen you.

However, it seemed my luck was beginning to change as I was still all alone at the dump station, at least for now. Thank goodness for small mercies! But clearly there was no time to lose.

Grabbing a nearby hose, no doubt put in that precise location for that exact purpose, I thoroughly diluted the lake through several minutes of high pressure dousing. But try as I might, the lingering, less-than-pleasant odor persisted and was likely to do so for quite some time before slowly dissipating.

Then, at long last, my thoughts could turn to my second shower of this still-young day. But after being told in no uncertain terms that I and my accompanying stench were both persona non grata inside the rig, a new set of clothes, toiletries kit and a large plastic bag for the old clothes were tossed long distance to me as I festered outside in the now blazing sun. I tell you true: no shower has ever felt quite that good, as I luxuriated under mounds of suds dwelling on a disaster and lessons I'm not likely to forget for a long, long time.

They say bad things generally come in threes. But while we can't prove the truthfulness of that warning, we can indeed vouch that nasties at least come in twos, and in very quick order to boot!

You see, about three hours later, we decided to stop for lunch at picturesque Thompson Pass, about 40 miles from Valdez. Afterwards, we took an extended walk before jumping into Bridget and heading off down the steep and winding road.

About five miles later, Suzanne wanted to take some videos on the fly. Rolling down the window, we were greeted by a noise so loud and grating we knew immediately it just couldn't be our lovely, oh-so-quiet diesel engine. I mean this was a sound loud enough to wake the dead!

What the heck could it be? Was it a loose muffler dragging underneath? Had a tire come loose? All sorts of apocalyptical thoughts went zooming through our minds, especially given the events of the all-too-recent past.

Hey, this was surely not the time to be playing 20 questions! So there was just one way to solve the day's second riddle—pull over and find out!

Guess what? Maughan had struck again. I had left our scissor-type back steps down and the sound we were hearing was them dragging along the ground behind us as we careened down through the steep pass. Right now in this narrative, I'm sorely tempted to switch to the imperial, all-encompassing pronoun "we," rather than the more accurate, but more embarrassing, "I." But it's time to call a spade a shovel or something like that!

Anyway, the steps were stretched out as stiff as a board, with their characteristic flexibility totally eliminated! What's more, in just that relatively short period of time, we (there's such sweet anonymity in pronouns!) had managed to wear down the bottom step a full quarter-inch or so.

The author planting a big smooch on a fair size
halibut on the docks in Valdez, Alaska.

And talk about friction. Luckily I had remembered to put on
my work gloves before examining the bottom rung, as the heat

generated by the prolonged rubbing of metal on road pavement was evident even through the heavy duty canvas.

But, apart from that, nothing else appeared to be irreparably damaged, except possibly my ego, confidence and self-esteem, which were in full meltdown mode, given this episode and the "sewer line caper" of just a few hours earlier!

This, however, was certainly not the time or place for my mechanically adept wife to begin any repairs. So quickly undoing the steps, again with the embarrassing factor in mind, I carefully placed them in the camper hallway, before proceeding on to Valdez, fully expecting unlucky number three to rear its ugly head at any moment.

Reaching beautiful Valdez, with no further incidents, we quickly checked into a campground located opposite the picturesque harbor area. Even though this turned out to be the best campground available by far, in truth the main emphasis was clearly on getting somewhere, anywhere in fact, as quickly as possible.

Given the "sewer caper" and subsequent "hot steps escapade", we, not just I, no longer felt certain that disaster number three wasn't lurking right around the next corner, just waiting to jump up and bite us you know where! Pure and simple, I just didn't want to tempt fate, even though we're certainly not superstitious.

But just to be on the safe side, pass over that four-leaf clover and the rabbit's foot, if you please. And how about throwing a pinch of salt over your left shoulder and touching our wooden table a few times just for luck. After all, one can't be too cautious, right?

27

CAP'N HOOK

CAP'N HOOK—OR is it Cap'n Courageous? Mike McKem certainly qualifies in both regards. As one might expect, in many ways Mike is your archetypal skipper. As we learned even before boarding his vessel, Cap'n Mike, as he likes to be called, possessed not only a jaunty air of confidence but, equally important, a voluminous knowledge of the sea and the creatures living under its surface. Prerequisites, I'd say, for his duties aboard the whale watching cruise vessel Renown, which plies the waters of Resurrection Bay off of Seward, Alaska.

Mike's also a guy who won't take no for an answer. You see, he's not only great at his job but he performs his duties with two artificial arms. In fact, you haven't lived until you've witnessed Mike steer a course with his feet and perform all manner of other intricate nautical chores using pincers instead of hands and fingers.

Way back when, at the age of 16, Mike was working on a farm in his home state of Oregon. He was also a volunteer fire fighter and was severely burned after being trapped between the original forest fire he was helping fight and the deliberately-set back burn.

Doctors had no choice but to amputate one arm. And the

way Mike tells it, the second one could have been saved but it proved so bothersome that he asked for it to be removed as well. The logic of removing, rather than saving, the second arm escapes me. But Mike assured me that there were compelling medical reasons supporting that most drastic decision.

That was many years and many adventures ago. Since that time, Mike has pursued successful careers as a race car driver, international yachtsman, commercial fisherman and charter skipper, his current occupation.

But for seven long years Mike was thwarted in his ambition to show visitors the wonders off the coast of Alaska's Kenai Peninsula. Citing safety concerns, the U.S. Coast Guard steadfastly refused to license him. But every turndown only fueled his determination not to be denied and, in the end, the authorities relented and the rest, as they say, is an incident-free history.

Cruise goers can always count on being treated to a heavy dose of Mike's salty wit, which only adds to the overall caricature of the aging sea dog. Talk about a benign version of Captain Long John Silver in Robert Louis Stevenson's much-beloved Treasure Island!

But don't let Cap'n Mike fool you. Beneath that rather rough, barnacled exterior lies the proverbial heart of Alaskan gold. Case in point. As youngsters are wont to do in such circumstances, one especially precocious young girl asked Cap'n Mike if she could steer the boat. Mike's immediate and somewhat predictable answer was an emphatic no.

But as we were ending our eight-hour voyage and heading back to Seward, he sought out the young girl and asked her if she'd like to take over the vessel. Of course her answer was a delighted and excited yes. And before docking, a string of other wannabe captains had also taken over the boat, much to everyone's delight.

Afterwards Mike was heard to say: "Kids. Never much cared for 'em!!!" Yeah, Mike, we know. Shakespeare had you pegged for sure when he penned the expression, "he doth protest too much."

Mike's vast knowledge of this entire stretch of Alaska's Kenai Peninsula proved a boon. Not only did we see the usual assortment of bird life, most notably the clownish puffins, but we also got up close and personal with what Mike described as a family of three whales that frequent a certain bay at that time of year.

We also encountered a sea otter taking a snooze on his back while riding the gentle waves and a small pod of porpoises that put on an acrobatic act around the bow before getting bored with our comparatively slow-moving craft. In addition, Mike maneuvered us closer and stayed longer than competing tour boats in front of the calving Holgate Glacier in Kenai Fjords National Park.

The majestic fjords were originally scoured out by other equally mighty retreating glaciers of yesteryear. What we saw of Holgate Glacier was just one minuscule part of the park, which covers a little more than 600,000 acres.

One of the park's more dominant features is the Harding Icefield, a 300-square-mile vestige of the last Ice Age. But like many beauties, it asks much before revealing itself. So as much as we would have loved to visit, we had neither the energy nor time to take the strenuous all-day hike from the base of Exit Glacier. But there's always next time.

Viewing the Holgate Glacier proved a bittersweet experience. On the one hand, getting this close to such a monstrous bluish-green mass was a never-to-be-forgotten experience accentuated by what sounded like rifle shots as cracks preceded massive chunks of blue-white ice crashing into the sea. But make no mistake about it, ours was a death watch, as warmer temperatures cause this and other glaciers worldwide to recede eventually into oblivion. Mike has been watching this particular glacier for about 30 years now and in that time it has drawn back about 100 yards from where it used to be joined with a sister glacier.

Did we get our money's worth? You bet we did—and in more ways than one.

What we saw out on the waters of Resurrection Bay was more or less predictable. But what we witnessed on board the Renown was ultimately just as memorable. For eight hours we got to watch Cap'n Mike, the personification of courage, skill and determination.

Mike McKem deserves our admiration, certainly not our pity, not so much for his obvious disability but for his steadfast will not only to overcome but also to excel. Thanks, Cap'n Mike. We did indeed have "one whale of a time"—as suggested on the promotional tee shirts given out after docking.

28

THINGS ARE LOOKING UP...

... WAY, way up!" I like to call it the upturned chin test. There's
nothing scientific about it. In fact, it's just a little something I
came up with during our years of bumming around the globe
as tourists.

Here's how it works, in theory at least. The higher the
mountain, the higher the chin must be raised to see the top.
That's it! I told you it was as unscientific as you can get. But
sometimes it's a case of simpler being better.

I can tell you that the last place we really got to test it out
was at Alaska's Denali National Park and Preserve. There, during that initial very special occasion, my chin first went up to
its usual mountain viewing position. But to my amazement I
found out that wasn't nearly high enough. So up, up and up it
had to go in order to fully take in Mt. McKinley, or Denali, as
it's known in these parts.

This is one humongous mountain. And that simple assessment comes from folks who've seen their share of impressive
peaks! To my mind, what makes Denali's grandeur all the
more attention grabbing is the fact that it doesn't have to vie

for prominence with other peaks as Everest has to with K2, Annapurna and a whole range of equally impressive contenders. Denali just sits there, on its lonesome, demanding to be admired in almost reverential terms for its own self and not as part of a package.

The Denali experience is like so many others in life. We've all listened as friends fervently tried describing some awe-inspiring natural wonder until they're almost blue in the face. But try as they might, until you actually get up close and personal with that experience yourself, it remains theirs and not yours. Seeing it in person adds that unbeatable extra dimension, somehow allowing you to take personal possession of it, while archiving it in your own memory.

That's how it was for us, not only with the Denali experience, but also in earlier years while viewing several other of the world's natural wonders, such as the Egyptian Pyramids, the Victoria Falls in Zimbabwe and Switzerland's grand peak, the Matterhorn. In fact, my memories remain most vivid and time resistant when I think of that first glimpse of the Pyramids and accompanying Sphinx. As we drove our Volkswagen camper bus along that Egyptian desert road from the port city of Alexandria towards Cairo, we came up over a rise and, as a total surprise, there they were.

And what a setting for Denali—its own national park larger than the state of Massachusetts. Stop and think about that for a moment. A national park bigger than the entire state of Massachusetts, which, after all, is no Rhode Island or Delaware when it comes to size.

But even with that huge space, it had become obvious that the ecosystems immediately surrounding Denali were in serious danger of being loved to death by the increasing number of adoring fans crushing into the park to add it to their list.

Without going into detail, I must say I like the system of

busing folks around Denali instead of the earlier unfettered automobile access to the park's limited number of roads. Cynically, it could be said that the relatively new system represents nothing more than a money grab by the US Park Service, the folks in charge of running and maintaining that huge piece of real estate.

But that would be to miss several salient points. First, when you look at the fees charged for what you get, it's actually good value for the money. And secondly, when you add to that the fact that the profits go towards defraying the significant costs of running such a sizable park, it's a slam dunk.

However, possibly the best justification is that the highly innovative and, for the most part, smoothly operating people-moving system has greatly relieved the human pressure on the park's diverse and extremely fragile environment. In fact, by all independent accounts, the system, begun only a few years back on an experimental basis, has been an overwhelming success.

A la Greyhound's suggestion that we leave the driving to them, what's not to like? For a reasonable fee you get a capable driver, totally conversant with the terrain, which, while being incredibly lovely, can and does show its teeth at times in the form of hairpin turns, some extremely narrow roads and one-way stretches that appear seemingly out of nowhere.

In addition, most of the drivers do an excellent job doubling as guides, naturalists, raconteurs and, in the case of ours in particular, humorists of considerable talent. It's as if these drivers, not quite ready for prime time but with captive audiences on board, spend an entire Alaskan summer honing their shtick while waiting to be discovered.

So given all the above, why should my verdict be anything less than an enthusiastic thumbs way up for the highly enjoyable, stress free, eight hours spent aboard our bus as we bumped and rumbled along unpaved roads designed to blend in as unobtrusively as possible with the natural surroundings.

If you wanted to just sit back and ooh and aah at the awe-inspiring scenery that greeted us around every bend, you were perfectly free to do so. If your thing was to be the first to spot some sort of exotic animal off in the far distance and then triumphantly announce it to your fellow passengers, then you could do that as well. And if you simply wanted to catch 40 winks, then that, too, was fine and dandy.

I'm rather glad individuality reigned supreme as clearly not everyone's sole reason for taking the trip was animal spotting. I'm glad because to be perfectly honest, if the trip's success rose or fell solely on the amount of wildlife sighted, it would have been judged marginally successful at best.

What wildlife we did see was, for the most part, far away and only visible with the aid of strong binoculars. And I mean strong! In the end, our driver's candid assessment was that we had had an average day with a small number of grizzlies, dall sheep, caribou, gyr falcon, golden eagle and Alaska's state bird, the ptarmigan, definitely identified.

Don't get me wrong, seeing even that small amount of wild-life was terrific, even if, for many, a strong imagination was a definite asset. But from my perspective, the highlight was never going to be the animals, even if they had come up and posed for us right next to the bus. It was always going to be the sheer size, breadth and glory of the park, especially when one considers that our day's journey probably only took us the equivalent of a round trip between Boston and Worcester, a distance of 100 miles at best.

If a sense of humility and reverence in the face of God's magnificent handiwork is not first and foremost on your mind during such an experience, let's just agree to disagree on that point. And as if that weren't enough, the day was topped off by THE mountain that makes all it surveys bow before it. To say Denali dominates all it surrounds is like saying Babe Ruth was a great baseball player. Enough said.

I'd like to be able to say that we saw Mt. McKinley in all its glory. However, for most of our visit, this peak of 20,320 feet hid from us, giving random glimpses from behind the clinging clouds.

But as frustratingly brief as those glimpses were, they were more than enough to confirm that this is a peak of uncommon grandeur, not to mention its height and overall size. In fact, we were told that Denali is so massive that it creates its own weather system. And here's another little fact to chew on: the only Alaskan glaciers continuing to grow in size are the 11 huge ones located within that specialized weather pattern.

When not touring the park and enjoying all the wonders it has to offer, the thousands upon thousands of visitors have to be housed, fed, entertained and otherwise relieved of large sums of cash. This is the job of the many businesses, large and small, that congregate along the Parks Highway that runs by the park entrance.

We RVers are somewhat insulated from this overpriced on-slaught and can limit the financial damage to our wallets, given that we carry our homes on our backs, so to speak. Still, RVers visiting Denali for the first time can find themselves suscepti-ble, especially if they've failed to stock up as much as possible on essentials ahead of time.

Being a strong believer in the free market philosophy, I cer-tainly have nothing against someone making a legal buck or two. Good luck to them.

Having said that, my only wish is that they'd take a little more time to be friendly during the process of separating you from your money. After all, a smile goes a long way. But I guess when you have only three plus months of summer to maximize profits, it unfortunately doesn't leave much time for life's niceties.

Our Denali experience also included a rather expensive evening out at a local dinner theater, which, as it unfortunately turned out, proved to be a stretch on both counts. At the risk of continuing to sound like a curmudgeon, the dinner was little more than a combination of not-the-freshest salmon and so-so pork ribs, followed by a cute but predictable vaudeville act about Alaska.

Okay, okay, maybe the theater part of it was a little more than cute and when we decided to get on with the program and go with the flow, I must confess that we did indeed have a fun evening. So in retrospect maybe what I'm really objecting to here is more my dislike of being treated not as an individual but as part of a herd to be moved in and moved out as quickly as possible.

In my mind's eye, I couldn't help but conjure up visions of some sharp, avaricious business types sitting around figuring out how best to part hapless touristos from as much money as possible while giving them a hyped up, dumbed down, version of Alaska in the cheapest way possible. Hey, maybe I'm just getting old and cynical.

So from my perspective when we "do" Denali again it will be with one thing and one thing alone in mind—to re-visit Alaska's crown jewel of parks and hopefully get better acquainted with its reigning royalty. Bring on the vagaries of nature's rain and mountain-obscuring clouds. No problem. We can handle that. That's the luck of the tourist draw.

We'll also do our best to avoid the man-made gauntlet of plastic vulgarities one has to run leading to the park. To my mind, at least, that only tends to detract what folks come to the park to experience in the first place. But obviously folks sharing my view are in the small minority, given the unbridled entrepreneurship on display just adjacent to the park's boundaries.

Well it's time now to move on to new adventures awaiting us down the road. But before we leave, let's see if there are any essential supplies we need to buy on our way out of town.

Oh yes, I almost forgot. We just have to get a few of those Denali Hawaiian dolls wearing those bright green hula skirts! The folks back in Australia will love them. How about six of those bright red "Denali Or Bust" tee shirts for the kids. And while we're here, we might as well get a few complete sets of bobble head Alaskan animals... those wind up growling grizzly puppets are cute... and how about those...

I hear what you're calling me. But it's "Mr." Hypocrite to you, if you please. Oh heck, no use getting all defensive about it because you're probably right. But, to be as fair as possible, I've always had the philosophy that if you can't beat them you might as well join in the fun! After all, I'm only human.

29

FORTY MILES OF BAD ROAD PLUS

FIVE PLUS hours to drive 114 miles. Come to think of it, that's about what we averaged many a day in our Volkswagen camper bus during our African odyssey from Addis Ababa to Cape Town in the early 1970s.

But we're not talking Africa here, folks. What we're in fact describing are conditions on Alaska's Denali Highway, which runs just over 135 miles between the George Parks Highway in the west to the town of Paxton at the junction of the Richardson Highway (Alaska Route Four) in the east. Or vice versa if you like, as they do allow you to start at either end!

Now let's be perfectly honest here. Rechecking the AAA map we used at the time, I note that the Denali Highway is clearly colored grey, as opposed to red, which indicates the more major roads. So right off the bat, that should tell any experienced map reader that if the decision is made to drive that road, it might not turn out to be a stroll in the park.

In fact, travelers using this secondary road can almost certainly count on unsealed and possible gravelly driving conditions for all but 25 miles and all the care, aggravation and extra time that entails. In other words, this is a road not to be driven without due consideration of the possible perils involved.

What's more, it should be noted that we took that length of time to get to our destination because we wanted to. If we had chosen to, we could have put the pedal to the metal, so to speak, and zoomed along at 30 or even 40 miles per hour. No 20 miles per hour speed limit signs here. In fact, there were no posted speed limits, period.

During our time in Alaska, Yukon and elsewhere I can't count the number of times we've been left in the dust and occasionally sprayed with road debris by RV brothers and sisters careening down roads helter-skelter in their rigs, hell bent on reaching some destination like yesterday. And I invariably find myself wondering where the fire is and why so many summer visitors to Alaska can't slow down and smell the lupines.

Thank goodness, most of the time, occupants and machines survive such driving excesses unscathed. But every now and then Mario and Mrs. Andretti get their just desserts and learn a very expensive lesson about driving for conditions. To their chagrin and dented wallets, they learn that even the strongest of metals can break when put under enough stress—and sometimes with disastrous consequences.

I'll tell you one thing, the Denali Highway tests your patience. On more than one occasion I found myself questioning whether we'd ever see the last of the seemingly endless potholes and wash-boarded sections. And to wile away the hours I had plenty of time to try to resolve the age-old argument over what driving strategy is better when it comes to wash-boarding.

You've heard the two ardently-held theories. Is it better to go very slowly, thereby giving your rig a better chance to survive intact but nearly shaking the fillings out of your teeth in the process? Or is it preferable to smooth things out by zooming over these corrugated sections at highly exaggerated speeds?

I've tried them both and frankly I definitely prefer paying the price of loose fillings to the downright frightening feeling of driving on something akin to slippery ice. I know it might sound downright old-fashioned, but I find my nerves to be much less jangled when we have the rig under some sort of control at all times. I'm funny that way!

The driving might have been tedious and all consuming, but our snail's pace at least afforded us the benefit of plenty of time to marvel at another day of unparalleled scenery. Like most visitors to Alaska, I'm running out of superlatives to describe the physical beauty surrounding us. So with that in mind, I've decided to eliminate "unparalleled" from my vocabulary, at least until we leave our 49th state.

Our decidedly less frenetic pace also allowed us to experience what I like to call the delicious serendipities of life. Try these on for size: watching a pair of swans and their four cygnets peacefully swimming on a small glacial lake; flushing a ptarmigan from its hiding spot by the side of the road; getting a good close-up look at a black porcupine as it lumbered along in front of us; and sharing our lunch with a marmot, also known as a prairie dog. I'm sure you'd agree that it doesn't always have to be the spectacular to delight the soul and fill the memory banks.

So with all this going on, it was rather late when we finally reached the BLM (Bureau of Land Management) campground at Round Tangle Lake, one of several lakes so named because they all seemed to be tangled together. At least that's the explanation offered and it sounds good to me.

Being self-contained is always a plus in Alaska and so it was again this evening. Since the campground was free of charge, there were no facilities other than a couple of strategically placed outhouses. You just drove out into the BLM area and picked an impromptu site.

In fact the only rule, and an unwritten one at that, was to observe the unofficial courtesy of not parking cheek by jowl with your neighbor. By all means, walk over and visit after you're all settled in. Some of our best friendships have been made that way. But, for goodness sakes, give your fellow campers some room. After all, I think you'd agree if there's one state large enough to spread out in, it's Alaska!

You'd be amazed how many times we've seen folks with vast amounts of empty space at their disposal plop themselves down almost on top of perfect strangers without seemingly thinking anything amiss. I can only guess they've heard one too many bloodcurdling stories of man-eating bears and moose!

Despite the seemingly endless variety of potholes and wash boarding, all would have been picture perfect on the Denali had the weather cooperated. Being cloudy and rainy all day did have the desired effect of keeping the dust down. On the downside, however, we instead had to contend with reduced traction in spots and a fine coating of mud liberally distributed all over Bridget, changing her white color to a chocolate brown. Now I know why those hot pressure-washing centers do such a land office business.

Apart from the lovely scenery and the "delicious serendipities," the next nicest aspect of the day was the almost total absence of tour buses and motorhomes careening down the center of the road. Every now and then we'd meet a pickup truck, presumably driven by locals. And while they passed us going like a bat out of you know where, we at least felt they knew what they were doing. At least that's what I told myself, uncurling my white-knuckled fingers from around the steering wheel.

Would we take the Denali Highway again, knowing what we know now? You better believe it. As Alaska becomes increasingly tamed and civilized it's nice to know that such a "grey" road still exists. So let's hope that the next time we check the latest AAA map of Alaska, the Denali will still be there in grey, offering similar challenges...and delights...for all those adventuresome enough to drive it. After all, if all the challenges are taken out of driving to and around Alaska, why bother going there any more?

30

STRUNG OUT IN
ANDERSON

No, no, don't get the wrong idea. I'm no over-aged hippie hiding out in the backwoods of Alaska growing and smoking dope as part of an ongoing personal, never-ending battle, or even rebellion, against convention and the ubiquitous military-industrial complex.

Yes, I must admit that I'm old enough to remember first-hand the 1960s, when a relatively small but highly vocal and dedicated proportion of my generation rebelled against the despised "establishment." Flower power was all the rage, and even though I remained, for the most part, on the outside looking in, I must confess that some of the ideals espoused by 1960's pop artist, Scott McKenzie, in "If You're Going to San Francisco" remain with me still.

So if I'm not this dope-smoking hippie drop-out from the '60s then why, you might legitimately ask, am I strung out in Alaska? Would it help if I told you I was far from alone? Aah, one of those hippie communes, you say.

No, no, no, you've still got it all wrong. When I say we were not alone, I'm merely referring to the fact that Suzanne and I were among hundreds of fellow devotees attending the 13th Annual Bluegrass and Country Music Festival held one July weekend in the tiny town of Anderson, just 80 miles or so south of Fairbanks.

Now there are devotees and then there are devotees. Huh? No, I'm really not in that drug-induced haze, as you suspect. What I'm trying to explain to you is that it's relatively easy to be a fan when all the outdoor conditions are perfect, or at least tolerable. You know the drill—balmy weather, nary a blood-sucking insect in sight, and a bucolic scene complete with skies filled with either sunshine or stars, depending on the time of day.

Now try maintaining that very same passion and concentration on the music while being bombarded by intermittent and often torrential rain. Throw in hordes of bloodthirsty mosquitoes and other assorted biting and stinging critters venturing forth on the wing from nearby forests when the sun begins to dip below the horizon, and all the ingredients are assembled for not mere distraction but for true and unmitigated mental mayhem.

But I'm happy to report that these and other potential enjoyment busters never came close to disrupting the more than 25 hours of some of the best and most authentic bluegrass/country music Alaska has to offer. To be sure, the quality of musical artistry varied greatly from fairly roughhewn renderings to the ultra professional performances of the headliners. But judging by the applause and the appreciation shown all the musicians, this unevenness of performance was of minor consequence.

More importantly, this festival continues to provide the relatively small but rapidly growing number of Alaskan bluegrass/country musicians the chance to not only cut their teeth professionally but also to exchange musical experiences on and off stage with the more venerable acts among them. And all the while, we, the listeners, are the beneficiaries, listening to hour after hour of great music, when not swatting at the marauding insects or racing for cover under rain slickers, umbrellas or more unconventional coverings such as garbage bags, etc.

Barry and Suzanne enjoying the bluegrass and country music in the tiny town of Anderson, 80 miles south of Fairbanks, Alaska.

It seems hard to believe that just a few years back there were dire predictions about the future of bluegrass, especially in far-off Alaska. These self-appointed experts were almost falling over themselves to issue the opinion that not enough young musicians were taking up the musical genre and thus bluegrass music was doomed to go the way of the now-extinct Dodo of Mauritius and the giant Moa bird of New Zealand. Talk about these opinions being strictly for the birds!

If any of these "experts" are still clinging to such a fanciful notion, all they needed to do was talk to any number of youngsters making great music throughout this wonderful weekend. If they did, the inescapable fact would emerge front and center that the torch has been well and truly passed, not only here in Alaska, but in the lower forty-eight states as well.

In fact, one of the headline acts, Bearfoot Bluegrass, has nary a 30-year-old in it. And this was the rule, rather than the exception, with most of the Alaskan bands on the program.

As is generally the case, Bearfoot Bluegrass, like so many others, grew up in a hurry when they traveled to Colorado to perform at the prestigious and ultra-competitive Telluride Bluegrass Festival and came away winning the Best New Band competition. "That really helped put Alaskan bluegrass music on the map," said lead mandolin player, Jason Norris.

Sharing top billing with the kids was veteran bluegrass singer and songwriter, Ginger Boatwright. Ginger's based in Nashville and told a very appreciative audience that she loves coming to Alaska to help encourage the growth of bluegrass in the state. To that end, Ginger's impromptu band consisted of two Alaskans, Greg Booth on banjo and pedal steel guitar and his son Jason on bass.

The members of Ginger's band might have been relative strangers to the stage but you'd never have known it. The sound was seamless, energetic and highly polished, all qualities sewn together by the strong sinewy vocal style of Ms. Boatwright. She really knows how to sell a song and I particularly liked an autobiographical number called "Sipsey," which recalls her childhood in Alabama. And it seems Crystal Gayle, among others, shares my enthusiasm for that song, as she had plans to record it.

At many festivals there's a surprise package—an act that pops up and unexpectedly blows you away. At the Anderson Bluegrass/Country Festival that person was singer/songwriter extraordinaire, Mike Campbell. Mike's a mountain of a man with talent and a laugh to match. He can melt your heart with a tender love ballad but he's better known for his fun songs, with evocative titles as "Evil Freddy" and "Salmon Love."

But to truly appreciate Mike's particular brand of northland humor, go on out and buy one, or better still, all of his CDs. Be forewarned, get ready for some real belly laughs, compliments of a true Alaskan character. There's also a true honesty to Mike's music. There's no attempt to romanticize his Alaska. He just lays out life in the state as he sees it and leaves the rest up to you, the listener.

I came away from the festival with a feeling of genuine freshness. I enjoyed the fact that the music was, by and large, heart-felt and exuberant, which allowed me to get past the varying quality of the overall musical product.

But my reaction shouldn't come as a surprise. After all, if I had to choose one musical genre as truly embodying the Alaskan spirit of tough self-reliance and gritty creativity, then bluegrass/country would be it. From the music in Anderson emerged a sense of the incredibly beautiful but harsh land that is Alaska—an environment that demands much, while rewarding grudgingly.

These are uniquely dedicated musicians. Compared with their fellow musicians in the Lower Forty-Eight states, the rewards remain comparatively few, given the frustrations posed by Alaska's harsh weather and vast distances. Not only have they survived, but if the festival in Anderson is any indication, the Barefoot Bluegrass Band won't be the last to enrich the genre with its uniquely Alaskan sound.

31

LITTLE THINGS MEAN A LOT

SURELY THE more senior of you can remember '60s pop singer Kitty Kallen, she of the squeaky little voice and the perennially perky personality. Well, Kitty had it right when she sang that little things certainly do mean a lot, even though, unlike her, I'm not throwing kisses from across the room or telling someone they look nice when they're not.

What's more, these little things are most always right there for the viewing, unlike the Mt. McKinleys of this world, which are often shrouded in clouds and thus disappointingly out of sight. In fact, all you need to enter this realm is an inquisitive mind and the willingness to look down.

Having followed those instructions, a new world unfolds before your very eyes—a miniature realm abounding with tree seedlings, flowers, lichens, edible berries and, yes, even animal dung or scat, as it's called by the outdoors set here in Alaska. It's as if this tiny, unobserved world is trying to tell us a story if only we're willing to take the time and effort to unlock the secrets hidden within.

I took up the challenge shortly after stopping for a night

of boondocking (otherwise known as free camping) at a huge quarry pit near the junction of the Elliott and Dalton Highways, about 70 miles north of Fairbanks and just a scant 116 miles south of the fabled Arctic Circle.

I wish I knew why my attention was suddenly focused on the micro. Possibly it was a mental response to my witnessing the vastness of the Alaskan wilderness just moments before from the lofty vantage point of the quarry rim. I can recall experiencing acute feelings of insignificance as I scanned the surrounding forest that formed a sea of green on all sides, broken only by the skyline stretching off as if to infinity.

Finally, no tangible sign of man's interference with nature's reality except, that is, for our truck camper snugly parked on the quarry floor far, far below. But all too soon that intrusion on the unsullied would also be gone. So after necessarily being cheek and jowl with other like adventurers, it was as if we had finally been set free to have this particular piece of Alaska all to ourselves, at least for a few short hours.

I felt an acute sense of proprietorship of the sheer beauty of what lay around me, a feeling underscored by a penetrating quietness that blanketed, thus enhancing, the entire scene. As strange as it seems, silence has a sound all of its own and one that soon becomes quite addictive and charmingly alluring, if given half a chance.

However, as I was to discover, the world around my feet was no less beautiful. Although it was only the first week of August, some of the ground cover was already turning myriad shades of autumnal colors in visual recognition of the winter that surely would come... and relatively soon by Alaskan standards.

But the lichens and moss that clung to the outcroppings of granite were less governed by the passing of the seasons. Their more somber colors of muted greens, grays and light browns would see them nicely through the winter unchanged, as they had done countless times before.

I had only to change the landscape by the brush of a hand or the sweep of a foot and some small creature's entire universe was disturbed or possibly gone forever. Ants were busy doing what ants do best—laying in stores, somehow knowing full well that in less than a month a significant amount of snow could be falling throughout this area, accompanied by plummeting temperatures that reach a balmy 50 below zero Fahrenheit! And a myriad of other insects, large and small, were following the example of the industrious ants.

Elsewhere, small mounds of scat gave evidence that larger animals had also gazed out upon this bucolic scene. And not so very long ago, judging by the state of the droppings. And in that scat was evidence of the ongoing struggle for survival that has been on going since time immemorial. Fragments of bone and scattered pieces of hair and fur bore silent witness to a brief, and ultimately futile, struggle against a bigger, more powerful foe.

Since the surrounding bushes still bore copious amounts of berries and the grasses a summer's growth of seeds, I could see that this area provided an ideal place of ambush. All the attacker, be it marten, weasel or the like, would have had to do was to crouch and wait, knowing that the lure of delicious berries and seeds would, in turn, provide a tasty meal of rodents, such as mice, voles, etc.

For many creatures, the place of my contemplation encompassed their entire universe—the place where they were born, lived, procreated, and, just possibly, as the bones and fur in the scat indicated, died. One could only imagine what untold dramas had been played out along this very quarry rim, not only over the centuries, but also in the relatively recent past. And all that's needed to enter this realm is a fertile imagination and a keen sense of observation!

Manley Hot Springs was 80 miles further along the Elliott and not exactly on the main tourist trail. Thank goodness for small mercies.

From here on out, the road promised to be more of the same—dusty gravel with the constant threat of cracked windshields from rocks thrown up by the infrequent, but always cannonballing, trucks and cars. I must say most Alaskans don't let little things like potholes and gravely, wash-boarded roads slow them down. In fact, they seem to revel in the conditions while putting the pedal to the metal!

We had a great time in Fairbanks, a city of just over 30,000—just big enough to have the wide range of goods and services you need, but small enough to afford ease of access.

Having said that, it was still wonderful to get back into what we consider the true Alaska—the seemingly endless tundra, interspersed with black spruce and light green aspens.

Manley Hot Springs came highly recommended, not so much by the tourist literature, but by those fellow RVers sharing our love of the unusual and the off-the-beaten-track sense of adventure. So with that in mind, it didn't take too much coaxing to lure us out into the wilderness again.

As strange as it might sound, we really didn't care what we did or did not find at the end of the Elliott Highway. We had been told that soaking in the local hot springs was quite restorative. And the woman who ran the local roadhouse was said to make a mean fruit pie. We'll investigate both for sure, but beyond that we'll just poke around and see what other big, but mostly small, adventures find us. Therein lies the true joy of our brand of RVing, stumbling on the truly serendipitous.

Yes indeed, Kitty Kallen, little things surely do mean a lot. But right now I was thinking of another of my favorite singers, the late Jim Croce. It's times like this that we shared Jim's sentiment about capturing time in a bottle.

When folks ask us where we're going to spend the coming winter I can't help but feel they're getting ahead of the game. That will take care of itself. It's the here and now that needs our full attention, lest it be squandered, leaving us with nothing to show for its passing.

Every day Alaska is proving more and more of a revelation. For starters, it's not nearly as crowded as we envisioned. I don't know what we expected. Maybe the emphasis on the main tourist attractions gave us a false sense that the state was, in fact, filled to the brim with out-of-towners during the relatively brief summer period.

But with the help of countless little things to see and do along the way and with a spirit of always trying to capture time in a bottle, Alaska will continue to fascinate us—that is, if we don't forget to look down in addition to up and around.

32

EIGHT CARS IN 160 MILES

NOW THIS is my kind of Alaska! You know, the mythical land of my Australian youth. A land my dreams told me was filled with Polar bears, Eskimos and Siberian huskies and where sun-lit nights gave everyday folks that extra time to scoop up those thousands upon thousands of huge gold nuggets just lying there for the taking in every river, stream and creek!

Ah yes, the world's last frontier—the land of Nanook of the North and Sergeant Preston, that is, if you're willing to overlook the teeny weeny little fact that both those two 1960s television heroes were actually Canadian, not Alaskan. But let's not split hairs, as I'm sure those two heroic purveyors of justice crossed the border in pursuit of the bad guys every now and then. And that was good enough for me!

All these images, plus many more, were dancing around my brain as we drove the approximately 80 miles of dirt road that began at the crossing of the Elliott and Dalton Highways. At that point, the Elliott headed west, south west and the Dalton due north to the town of Deadhorse, the northernmost termi-nus of the famed Trans-Alaska pipeline and 10 miles inland from the once-tremendous oil field at Prudhoe Bay.

Rush hour in northern Alaska!

Our destination was the tiny town of Manley Hot Springs—the westernmost terminus of the Elliott. Enveloped in dust and with our tires playing dodge 'ems with sizable potholes, we didn't know whether to thank or curse the young couple from Spokane, Washington, who had described Manley as a "can't miss" sort of place.

Not knowing exactly what that meant, and being reluctant to challenge their assessment, we decided, nonetheless, to give it a bash, even though it wasn't exactly on the road to anywhere else. But, then again, we reasoned, that also can be said about lots of other wonderful Alaskan destinations.

We also remembered the young couple extolling the beauty of the scenery along the Elliott, while making special note of the friendly folks living in Manley. Once again, in all fairness, that description could also apply to most places in the 49th state. But then came the clincher: Manley Hot Springs contained virtually no tourists or RVs.

All right! Suddenly Manley Hot Springs had become an official part of the Maughan itinerary. Now don't get us wrong. It's not that we don't like our fellow RVers. Why, just the opposite is true. No one likes a good yak better than yours truly, but there are limits.

We've always enjoyed being loners, with the timetable and course being our own and not some compromise. Call it the Africa syndrome – a reference to our previously mentioned overland trip from Ethiopia to South Africa with a one year old in tow! Yes, Kevin did survive, and no, we wouldn't even consider making such a trip again nowadays, not for a million dollars!

Much of Africa's allure was its wide and untamed open spaces. Likewise, the road to Manley Hot Springs offered some of the wildest, most starkly beautiful countryside Alaska had offered us to date.

The Elliott plunged across the top of some rather impressive mountains framed by forests of the ubiquitous Black Spruce as far as the eye could see. And, for the most part, we had this splendid scene all to ourselves, rarely seeing another car going in either direction during the entire three-hour drive.

It takes a lot to impress us as travelers. But impressed we most certainly were when we finally pulled into this metropolis of less than 100 souls.

Can't say exactly what turned us on. Maybe it was the all-pervading quiet. More likely, though, we recognized that Manley Hot Springs was already living up to its reputation of being a "pocket of pioneer Alaska."

I was purposely vague when tallying up the town's current population because, depending on whom you talk to, it ranges between a low of 64 and a high of 94. But there is consensus on one unfortunate fact: the population of Manley Hot Springs is dropping. And the reasons had an all-too-familiar Alaskan ring to them: low world gold prices, extremely high fuel prices and tighter fishing regulations.

The net result: lots of women out looking for good men, most of whom are off somewhere else looking for work, first and foremost, and female companionship only after the fact! And the eligible men still around town (read that upright and breathing) aren't exactly the cream of the crop, if you can believe the candid assessment of two self-described "man hungry" females we met at Manley's main watering hole, the Manley Roadhouse.

In fact, they told me they had had to resort to employing the "catch and release" policy, the local quality being so poor! They also said when it came to hooking one of these male leftovers, "The odds were good but the goods were definitely odd!"

I'm still trying to figure out their exact meaning, daring not to ask these two man hunters at the time and preferring not to broach the subject later with my good wife! You know the old adage, "If you really don't want to hear the answer, then it's best not to ask the question!"

So I could predict, with a great degree of certainty, that the fast-approaching winter was going to be extra, extra cold for some of the good women of Manley! And this in an area where temperatures regularly get down to as low as 50 degrees below zero Fahrenheit!

One longtime resident of Manley Hot Springs was Gladys Darte, who, at 80-plus years, showed no sign of slowing down or giving in to the harsh environment. She and husband Chuck owned the Manley Hot Springs (now there's a unique name!), but unless one of the locals told you where to look, I can almost guarantee you'd have never found it. No signs, no nothing, anonymity in keeping with their attitude that those really interested in soaking their bodies would ferret out their house.

We did, after some admitted fits and starts, and were treated to more than an hour of lolling around in decadent comfort in one of three eight by eight by four foot square concrete pools. The water in each was kept at a different temperature, with the coolest being around 100 degrees Fahrenheit and the hottest most likely used for boiling lobsters! We naturally chose the coolest, figuring we didn't travel all the way to Alaska to be boiled alive! The cost? The princely sum of five dollars each.

And in keeping with what we were now beginning to take for granted, the place was empty except for us. Now we fully understood why the reputation of Manley Hot Springs for tranquility had made the place so attractive to us in the first place.

Our luxurious private baths at Manley Hot Springs, Alaska.

Another enticing feature of the bathhouse was its location, inside a greenhouse alive with tropical vines, fruit, orchids and, as Suzanne spotted, a family of ermine. It was literally a tropical jungle right smack dab in the middle of Alaska! What's more, Gladys told us that it would stay that way throughout the winter, no matter the plummeting outside temperatures.

When our fingers and toes began looking like shriveled prunes, we dressed and sat a spell with Gladys and her friend Vera, who were locked in a titanic game of Scrabble. They looked up long enough to regale us with lots of great stories gathered during their 46 years in Manley.

Most were humorous but not all. Gladys related how she had lost a daughter and son-in-law two years ago in a local snowmobile accident. Then Vera told us how her 90-year-old husband Richard had died two weeks earlier, while still on the job delivering fuel, as he'd done for the past 50 years.

Vera and Gladys said it was not merely enough for "man hungry" women like the two at the Roadhouse just to bring their soft, feminine bodies to any union. That, they said, was a luxury reserved for the easier, less physically demanding, lifestyle of the Lower Forty-Eight, as rural Alaskans refer to the rest of the US.

Yes, next to their sled dogs, rural Alaskan men prized the softer, feminine qualities of their women. However, as Vera and Gladys explained it, the surest way for a woman to win the heart of an Alaskan man was to be not only soft and feminine, but also to be able to dress out a moose, chop up hundreds of Chum salmon to feed to the dogs and chop cord after cord of firewood. Sex, they said, was very, very low on the list of priorities and only indulged in when all those and countless other chores had been completed or when totally snowbound!

The social, gastronomical and economic heart of Manley Hot Springs was most definitely the Manley Roadhouse. Originally built in 1903, the roadhouse served as the town's lone and, I might add, excellent restaurant and hotel.

But it was much, much more. With pictures of the town's proud and often tumultuous history covering most of its walls, the roadhouse also served as the unofficial mecca, having a bar, a laundromat and a games area, complete with the usual billiards table, dart board, music machine and big-screen cable television.

Keeping the place warm when the inevitable howling winds and unbelievably low temperatures hit presented a major and ongoing problem. Burning up to a cord of wood a week certainly helped, but piping in hot air and water through underground lines really did the trick.

The source of all this heat was a huge furnace located adjacent to the roadhouse. Without this, the roadhouse would have had to close during the long winter months.

Gladys Darte also showed us another source of great wintertime warmth. It was an exquisite full-length coat made especially for her by an Eskimo friend in Nome. Made from the pelts of spotted seals fringed with beaver and lined with silk, it even looked warm from afar.

The secret was to keep the face warm, we were told. And the coat's protruding hood did just that. In fact, it could be folded in to protect the face even more when things really got nippy. Suzanne tried it on and said it was not only warm but surprisingly light.

On our first swing through town we decided to have lunch by the banks of the Tanana River, which was at flood stage due to heavy rain in its catchment basin and melting glacial snow. Exercising what we thought was extra cautious and prudent judgment, we parked our truck camper about 10 feet from the river's edge. That proved to be a much wiser move than we could ever have imagined.

As we stood outside our home on wheels admiring the awesome power of the river, huge chunks of the asphalt landing area were literally being devoured by the churning water before our very eyes. And, without exaggeration, by the time we got safely out of there, half of the asphalt between us and the river had already been consumed. I don't even want to think what could have happened if we had decided to camp in that spot for the night. We might well have woken up floating in the Bering Sea!

There was lots more of the town we would loved to have explored on foot. But word was already out that there was fresh Lower Forty-Eight meat in town, so the mosquitoes sent out a huge welcoming committee.

But we've vowed to fool them next time. Before even considering any second visit, we will have purchased two jackets with the hands and head area completely covered by fine mosquito-proof netting. Believe you me, we learned the hard way that such outdoor wear is an absolute must if you are to avoid literally being eaten alive by these voracious B-52s, armed with previously-noted prodigious hypodermic needles.

But, despite its quaintness, it was obvious that economic activity in Manley was slowly grinding to a halt. Oh yes, there were a couple of small charter businesses, but they appeared to be barely hanging on. As one would expect, given these conditions, we sensed growing resentment towards the state and federal governments, both of which were accused of being in the pocket of big business to the detriment of the small landowners.

Most locals railed against the "overfishing of salmon on the high seas and the growing environmental movement restricting their right to subsistence hunting." Was there a whiff of trouble in paradise? To my mind, it smelled more like the strong stench, not so much of smoldering resentment but of downright hostility. Unfortunately, we had encountered these very same sentiments in all too many Alaskan locales, with Manley Hot Springs being only the latest.

Given all this unhappiness, it shouldn't have surprised us to see several vehicles sporting bumper stickers supporting

Alaskan secession from the United States. No, I haven't been drinking more than my fair share of Grandma's elderberry wine. We were genuinely shocked to see them.

Granted, we saw less than a 100 of these stickers during our entire stay. And granted, there's always going to be a fringe element unhappy and dedicated enough to launch such a bumper sticker campaign. That's the beauty of a free and open society.

But dismissing the bumper stickers as merely the work of "kooks" would be to grossly underestimate Alaskans' fundamental love of independence and distrust of large government. After all, that's why many moved there in the first place! So we'd hope the government bureaucrats move to address these complaints before suddenly finding out that the dissatisfaction, so disdainfully dismissed, was much more Alaskan than ever imagined.

33

THERE'S GOLD IN DEM THAR HILLS...

FOR SOURDOUGH Jack Hendrickson and his family, it's never been a question of if the precious gold stuff exists on their parcel of land, but exactly where. And it's been this hauntingly tantalizing and thoroughly frustrating search that's proved a lifelong quest.

Jack's fully convinced (just ask him!) that his ticket to riches beyond compare can be punched if he and his family work just one more day and keep moving massive amounts of earth around their property. We found the Hendricksons not far from the Circle Hot Springs Resort and the thriving metropolis of Central, boasting a population of about 60.

But we were cautioned that Central's population tally is only an approximation. It seems there are more than one or two recalcitrant inhabitants living way back in the neighboring woods who just don't take too kindly to any government types poking around asking too many fool questions. Hey, I can understand that. After all, wasn't it this search for anonymity and privacy that drew these individuals to Alaska in the first place?

Like many first-time visitors to America's northernmost state, we wanted to experience the gold panning experience. After all, Alaska is almost synonymous with gold, so why not? But not at one of those crass commercial outfits that are seemingly around every bend in the road. If you've been to Alaska I'm sure you know the ones I'm referring to, where the panning dirt is salted with specks of gold dust to keep the tourists happy, no matter how fraudulently. That's show biz, I guess.

That's where Jack and his family come into the story. We were in the lobby of the Circle Hot Springs Resort admiring the lovely collection of photographs of the spectacular Northern Lights, otherwise known as the Aurora Borealis. What made them extra special is that most of them were taken from the front porch, just outside of where we were standing. What hauntingly beautiful colors and shapes! We're told these northern lights have to be seen in person to be fully admired and appreciated.

If you're interested, the Circle Hot Springs Resort actually contains a hot springs (surprise, surprise) which was used by the local Athabascan Indians long before the Gold Rush brought the interloping white men to the area in the 1890s. As its tourist brochure states: the Circle Hot Springs Resort offers year-round swimming, lodging, food and RV parking. The key word, to my mind at least, is year-round. Sorry, but the tourist brochure's tempting invitation notwithstanding, this is one RVer who is definitely not contemplating sampling the delights of the resort during an Alaskan winter, which, I'm told on good authority, tends to get a wee bit nippy! Would you believe down to 50 degrees below zero Fahrenheit nippy!

Anyway, we just happened to mention to the desk clerk that we might be interested in doing a little authentic gold panning—the real panning, we emphasized, and not the let's-make-the-tourist-happy roadside charades. The clerk said he had just the perfect spot in mind and promptly directed us to the Hendrickson's place a few miles down a dusty track.

We actually met Jack and one of his sons at an awkward time. You see, their base of operations was in the process of being moved further down the stream, where Jack was sure he stood a much greater chance of striking the elusive Mother Lode.

Anyone thinking such operations center around the romanticized pick and shovel would be sorely mistaken. Racer mining, as it's called, involves moving ton after ton of rocks and dirt by way of giant earth-moving equipment and then sifting it through a huge, very noisy, sluicer.

Another misconception is that good-sized nuggets (a dime to a quarter in size) are rather common. On the contrary, Jack told us that, in fact, he can count the number of nuggets he's found that size on one hand.

What they scrape out a living on are the so-called gold flakes and dust, which settle to the bottom of the sluicer. You see, gold is 19 times heavier than water, while rock is only six times heavier. And it's this type of gold that barely keeps them solvent after they pay for diesel fuel, mercury and other supplies.

Jack's your basic dreamer, and his seven children have all taken their turn helping him chase his dream. I asked him if his wife enjoyed the hunt for Eldorado and his rather terse reply spoke volumes: "She tolerates it."

Jack and his family have lived in the Alaskan bush for more than 20 years. After renting small places for most of their married life, Jack is particularly proud of the fact that he's now in the midst of having his own place built. When I asked him what he would do if he struck a large vein of gold, he said no one would ever know he'd found it because he wouldn't want the Alaskan and federal governments sinking their tax claws into him.

Feeling very lucky, Suzanne and I were given several rather heavy pans of dirt and rocks and pointed in the direction of a small pond. The object was to squat by the pond's edge and to shake the rocks and dirt around in the partially submerged top pan, which is purposely designed with several uniform holes in it. This allows the smaller pieces of dirt and gold nuggets to fall through the holes to the second pan below.

The author futilely panning for gold near Circle Hot Springs, Alaska.

Jack stood close by, giving instructions, moral support and encouragement that quickly turned to commiseration when we failed to find any color, to use the vernacular. Well, I must 'fess up because that's not exactly true. We did extract five specks of gold each smaller than one of the periods on this page. These were duly carefully stashed away in a small film case filled with water to be regularly admired by all, whether there was truly a desire or not.

The way I figure it, that's the least they can do given the

strenuous effort that went into wrenching those golden flecks from the Alaskan soil—an effort, I might add, that had me doubled over with sciatic back pain for several days thereafter.

Apart from considerable discomfort, the whole experience also cost us a total of 40 dollars, which we were more than willing to pay just to avoid being a part of the conveyor belt of gold panners at those other enterprises mentioned earlier.

Sensing we were a captive and empathetic audience, Jack began to vent some pent-up frustration against "the increasing number of EPA regulations on Alaskan gold mining." It's his contention that it's these and other unfriendly edicts that have caused the number of small family mining operations around Central to drop from more than 300 a decade ago to just a handful today.

Fair enough. While I'm all for free enterprise, I'm also against the poisoning of our natural resources with the irresponsible and thoroughly uncaring use of poisons such as mercury in mining operations. But that was not the time, or place, to begin such a philosophical conversation with Jack who was much bigger and stronger than yours truly!

Jack owns the land, patent rights and all, so he figures to be a gold miner for the rest of his life. Some of his children have grown and moved away. But there are still plenty left at home to help run the large earth-moving equipment and equally big sluicer.

After thanking him for his hospitality, we wished him good luck. And it wasn't said in a perfunctory manner as a way of ending a conversation. I truly hoped he would someday hit the long sought after but elusive Mother Lode. I admire folks who are willing to take a chance in life and not sit around waiting for a handout from the government or elsewhere.

So Jack Hendricksen, here's hoping that, in fact, there is gold, and lots of it, in not just dem thar hills—but in your hills!

34

BEEN THERE, DONE THAT!

AUTHOR'S NOTE:
ONE OF the bittersweet experiences associated with travel—and with life in general, for that matter—is that we find someone we enjoy, admire, even love, only to lose them. Such is the case of Harrie Hughes, the last remaining link with the region's wild and woolly gold rush days. Harrie died in June, 2006, after I wrote this chapter, but not before leaving us a lasting legacy to be treasured forever. So we salute Harrie for sharing his memories of those days—memories I related after a long conversation with him.

Still sharp of mind and intellect, 102-year-old Harrie Hughes holds forth in number seven cabin at the Circle Hot Springs Resort.

You see, Harrie's an Alaskan icon of sorts. He's one of the few remaining links with the wild legendary Gold Rush, which took place in both Alaska and the neighboring Canadian territory of the Yukon. Born on April 29, 1899, Harrie has witnessed three centuries and, to hear him talk, has done just about everything.

According to Harrie, he started out in Hollywood helping make silent movies. And, the way he tells it, he was the personal friend of that era's leading lights, Douglas Fairbanks, Jr., and Mary Pickford.

Jobs in construction, government espionage, and the Coast Guard followed. In fact, he says it was as a gunnery officer on board a naval patrol vessel that first brought him to the southern Alaskan port of Ketchikan. The rest, as they say, is history.

In his more than 50 years in Alaska, Harrie has been a trapper, a homesteader, a gold trader and about anything else, as he puts it, that would legally turn a dollar. He claims to have walked throughout the state from Nome to Valdez, most times blazing trails through the untamed wilderness as he went.

His walks are also said to have taken him to the gold mining mecca, Dawson, where he claims to have known the famous Klondike Kate. In fact, he told me in strictest confidence that Kate would, as he put it oh so delicately, only share her bodily favors with miners willing and able to pay her weight in gold dust.

On the subject of law and order, Harrie said the Alaskan police and the Canadian Mounties would only warn felons once to get out of town. If they didn't, he said, it was common knowledge that these lawbreakers were tossed into silt-laden rivers, their bodies dragging to the bottom, never to be seen again.

I looked for a twinkle in Harrie's eye as he related that story but saw none. In fact, as if to make his point, he assured me of the authenticity of what described as this "effective" system of justice.

Harrie thinks Alaska has gone to hell in a hand basket. On more than one occasion he roundly criticized the state politicians, calling them a bunch of crooks and deriding their knowledge of the "true Alaska." He never got around to specifically spelling out just exactly what he meant by the "true Alaska," so I'm left to ponder his precise meaning.

But one clue might be contained in his admonition of the Alaskan government to stop "screwing up" the lives of folks living in Alaska's interior with layer upon layer of bureaucratic red tape. And he bemoaned the "erosion of the last frontier."

Harrie's fundamental credo: treat your fellow man honestly and the land with respect and dignity. Simple values from a very uncomplicated man.

When asked how he managed to live so long, Harrie attributed his longevity to "booze in moderation, lots of hard physical work, healthy eating habits and good genes." And as if to emphasize that last point, he noted that his father had managed to live to be 102.

When pressed for more details on his eating habits, Harrie said he ate mostly caribou, moose, salmon and grayling, but never bear or lynx, which he described as scavengers and not worthy of being eaten. But he acknowledged that he'd met plenty of good men who had eaten and liked both.

Harrie's greatest frustration was no longer having the physical strength to match his mental abilities. He put it this way: "My mind says go but the body says no."

He loves visitors and will sit and chat for hours, as he did with Suzanne and me. There's no fear of losing his knowledge when he passes from the scene. He has a tape machine that has recorded his thoughts on virtually every subject.

We talked for nearly two hours nonstop and barely scratched the surface. But I'm thankful that long and winding conversation is now safely stored on our tape machine—that too for posterity. Then, all too soon, it was time for his nap, one of Harrie's few concessions to his advanced age.

From time to time, I can't help but think of that remarkable man and the invaluable contributions men like Harrie made to building today's Alaska. Yes, Harrie Hughes is a man not lacking in self-assurance. And upon reflection, it was probably that very same trait that most likely contributed to his successfully making his way in those less-than-genteel days.

I find in him a total absence of arrogance or cockiness. In fact, if I were forced to choose one term to describe this man it would be "matter of fact." Harrie just tells it like it was and lets the chips fall where they may. Harrie is devoid of embellishment. Come to think about it, I guess when you get to be his age, such adornment is hardly necessary!

Without a doubt, he has seen and experienced more of Alaska than almost any other living man. What's more, Harrie is quite secure, to the point of being downright proud of his contribution.

The term "living legend" is thrown around all too freely nowadays. But in Harrie's case, it fits like a glove. He's one of the very last links to a legendary golden age. I found it quite fitting that we had stumbled on this fantastic chance to meet Harrie Hughes, especially at a time when we were preparing to wind down our trip to this equally fantastic state.

Thanks, Harrie Hughes, and here's to another 102 years.

35

BEARS, MOOSE, WHALES AND OTHER CRITTERS

LET'S FACE it—a major part of the allure of traveling overland to Alaska, whether by the Stewart-Cassiar Highway or the better-known and more popular Alaska Highway, is the possibility of seeing lots of different and, dare we say, exotic wildlife along the way. But this expectation goes way beyond merely hoping to see the occasional unfamiliar critter, be it on land, sky or water. It's as if most travelers trekking north to Alaska expect a written "exotic wildlife viewing guarantee" to be included in the piles of maps, brochures and other travel goodies given out along the way.

We've actually heard of and indeed even spoken to RVers whose opinion of their Alaska trek was almost totally predicated on the number of beasties and birdies seen with their very own eyes. And definitely not good enough are the "I think I saw something with the shape of a bear in the woods over there" or "Look up there, I swear there was a large eagle-looking bird perched up in that tree a minute ago."

And these intrepid folks are not likely to be fobbed off with rabbits, squirrels or the like. After all, they certainly didn't travel thousands of miles and burn up who knows how many hundreds or even thousands of gallons of fuel to see species readily seen at home in Podunk or Evergreen or some other such locale in the Lower Forty-Eight.

No sirree, they're after bigger game, both literally and figuratively. And nothing less than the pantheon of critters synonymous with the Northlands will do. And we're talking bear, moose, bald eagles, whales and the like. What's more, the closer they are to you when viewed, the more bragging points you earn among fellow animal-spotting devotees. And if you truly want to administer the coup de grace, throw in sightings of other species, such as the elusive coyote, arctic fox or a caribou or two, for good measure. Now you're really on a roll!

In fact, one could go as far as to say there's this unspoken, yet very real, competitive streak in Alaska trek veterans when it comes to both the number of "exotics" actually seen and under what circumstances. Invariably campfire conversations get warmed up with brag sessions about how close this bear was or how many bald eagles were sitting on a particular tree. I tell you it gets so downright discouraging that when my turn comes to try and match or possibly top such visual exploits, I invariably find any excuse, including Mother Nature's call, to extricate myself from these Critter Sighting Olympics!

Upon reflection, I guess Suzanne and I saw our share of bear, moose, bald eagles, etc. But who knows? What's average, below average and above average? It's not as if there are scoreboards all along the major roads detailing the numbers of each critter to be seen in order to be considered average. I can see these billboards now… "Every month each tourist, to be considered average, must see 20 bears, 25 moose, 5 whales and 200 bald eagles."

Come to think of it, the job of posting such month-to-month numbers could fall to the various tourist entities in

British Columbia, Yukon and Alaska. Better still, why not form joint ventures with state, territorial and provincial mental health associations? The argument could certainly be made that such billboards would have the effect of relieving loads of pent-up angst, self-doubt, even rage among those animal spotters not knowing for sure if they had indeed made the grade. At the same time, those languishing in the below average range would receive a dubious sort of solace by receiving more proof positive that local tourist authorities were indeed in cahoots with tour book writers and others in hyping the "actual" numbers of critters to be seen.

They say confession is good for the soul. Well, if so, here goes. We went weeks before spotting our first moose, despite untold numbers of tantalizing signs tipping us off that the giant critters were all over the place. Maybe they were there—just out of eyesight but certainly not out of mind. In fact, every bend in the road was accompanied by the heart-pounding expectation of seeing not just any old moose but a huge, majestic one with a rack of antlers reaching to the sky! Boy, it's amazing how a prolonged sense of longing will play tricks with our expectations.

In fact, I was beginning to think this whole moose thing was just a scam designed to lure tourists up here. I began mentally exploring whether there were ways of demanding my money back on the grounds of false advertising! I defy you to drive more than 20 miles in most areas of British Columbia, Yukon or Alaska without seeing one of those road signs with a picture of a full-antlered moose on it warning that you are entering a moose crossing area. Now if that isn't a come-on, I don't know what is!

My moose mania got so bad that once when we visited a little museum we even found ourselves getting excited over a stuffed moose featured there. But even though I went into hyper rationalization mode, I knew deep down inside that a stuffed moose just wasn't a substitute for the real deal! To all those near me it appeared my condition was deteriorating—I needed a moose fix bad—and I needed it soon. At that point I had become so crazed and obsessed that I probably would have settled for some moose droppings! That'll give you an idea of just how desperate I was.

But then when we least expected it, it happened. We rounded a bend and surprised a cow browsing on the side of the road. And to our sheer delight and exceedingly good fortune, instead of hightailing it off into the woods, she decided to try and outrun us down the road. So we slowed down accordingly and for about a mile got this charming view of a moose's rear end before she decided enough was enough and veered off and rapidly disappeared into the nearby woods.

Curiously, we also found coyotes to be of great interest and the first one we spotted was busily eyeing its next meal by some railroad tracks. Suzanne characterized it as being a little motley looking, but I reminded her that Wily Coyote always had that same moth-eaten look as he unsuccessfully did battle with his arch nemesis, the Roadrunner. But what would she know, she never had a television as a child. Culturally deprived—that's what she was and is!

Suzanne did the honors by sighting our first bald eagle. At first glance I thought it was just another turkey vulture—so much for my birding skills. But after whipping out her binoculars, followed by her ever-ready Peterson's Guide to Birds of North America, my dear wife proved me wrong in no uncertain terms. We men should be used to that, shouldn't we? While sightings of bald eagles became almost commonplace, we never ceased to be thrilled by these magnificent, almost regal-looking birds, be they perched on a tree, soaring high overhead doing their thing on the thermal currents, or skimming above the water's surface about to take home a fresh salmon dinner.

The Lupine—a constant roadside companion
throughout most of the Pacific Northwest.

Through the unofficial but highly effective and generally reliable RV hotline we had heard that if bald eagles were your thing, then Haines, Alaska, was your place. We had seen pictures of scenes within its town limits showing baldies to be almost as numerous as pigeons in city squares. But nothing quite prepared us for the mind-boggling profusion of these huge birds in Haines. They were everywhere! Talk about sensory overload—there were literally hundreds of baldies perching on virtually every pole, tree and fence in town. And to think that just a relatively few years ago their southern cousins were hovering on the verge of extinction!

And Haines was to play a pivotal role in what was, in retrospect, the undoubted highlight of our animal sighting experience—during this particular trip, at least. There we sat in this lovely town voicing our usual lament of not seeing "our fair share of animals" to anyone who would sit still for a second. Finally some fellow touristos decided to take pity on these two whining old folks. They told us that each evening at a specific time and place along the Haines Highway, a mother grizzly bear and her cub would take up residence on the side of the highway for all and sundry to see, photograph and just simply admire.

Any normal folks would most likely have just said "Sure, sure" and written it off as another old wives' tale. But such was our desperation to see a living, breathing bear that we scheduled our return to Haines Junction, Yukon, in order to be at the appointed spot at the appointed time.

Lo and behold, when we arrived there were mother and second year cub busily grazing and doing whatever bears do and exactly, I mean exactly, in the appointed spot. Hallelujah! Out came camera and video camcorder and for the next half hour or so we and others were in bruin heaven, with ringside seats to the best darned bear show the Haines Highway had to offer.

But all good things must come to an end, and eventually Mama bear signaled she had had enough of all this gawking and photography by becoming visibly agitated. At that point we decided it was, after all, her territory and not ours, so off we went. Looking back, we realized the main reason for her irritation was her desire to cross the road in order to head on home to her den before nightfall. Talk about getting a trip's worth of bear watching in one sitting!

The only other "sure thing" in terms of animal spotting occurred several weeks later. We had stopped for diesel and were fortunate to get an attendant who, along with tending the pumps, also dispensed bits of local tourist information. Among many other things, he noted that a few kilometers further on (we were in Yukon), a group of mountain goats congregated at certain times of the day to lick salt off the side of the road.

We asked and received more specific directions but as it turned out we needn't have bothered. As was the case throughout our tour of the Northlands we saw the people watching the goats long before we were able to catch a fleeting glimpse of the goats themselves!

This brings to mind another tip for animal spotting—if there's a knot of cars, RVs and the like by the side of the road it's a good bet that some sort of "exotic" animal will be on view near by.

Come to think of it, that might be an excellent way of solving all this "animal angst" from the git go. I propose that local authorities humanely tether moose, bear or other "exotics" at various undisclosed locations along the side of all the major highways. In this way the average Mabel and Joe Tourist plus Barry and Suzanne could get their fill of animal sightings right off the bat, thus leaving their minds more receptive to focusing on the other reasons they expended all this time, energy and money in the first place.

But, then again, animal rights activists could make a compelling case that this would be cruel and unusual punishment for these poor animals. It would be argued with great conviction and persuasion that given their druthers, these and any other self-respecting members of Alaska's animal kingdom would rather not be caught anywhere near human habitation at any time from June through September.

Hey, better still, why doesn't the Disney Corporation or another one of those theme park operators just simply build a "Great Northlands" park, a la Walley World of "Summer Vacation" movie fame. It could come complete with plastic and plaster of Paris snowcapped mountains, evergreen trees, salmon-laden streams, cabins in the woods, bears, moose, whales, etc.

And the mind boggles at all the various rides that could be incorporated into such a park. How about a huge roller-coaster called "The Grizzly," a water slide named "The Slippery Salmon," or mechanical swings attached to a huge antlered moose? The possibilities are virtually limitless!

Not only would such a theme park save lots of folks the time and trouble of actually driving all that way north, this way these "intrepid" travelers could be guaranteed to see just as many exotic animals as they wanted, without any fear of disappointing the kiddies.

What's more, they would also have the convenience of buying all their souvenirs (for example, Mt. McKinley or Denali snow-globes) and food (think Salmon Burgers and Moose Chips) at one hassle-free stop. I mean this driving hundreds of miles from place to place collecting souvenirs at the actual site is such a drag, not to mention being a gross waste of time! Hey, there's such a thing as carrying this back-to-nature thing to illogical extremes.

By Jove, I think we have a winning idea here, as I'm sure lots of travelers, especially those with children, would simply love the idea of guaranteed animal sightings. Forget the teeny-weeny impediment that they'd be of the non-live, plastic variety. After all, you can't have everything. And do you think the younger ones will even notice that small detail?

And, you know what, I think I can guarantee the enthusiastic approval of many native northlanders, most notably the four-legged, finned and feathered variety.

This way they'd get a bigger dose of peace and quiet during the prime spring and summer months. After all, it gets a little old always having to wait for the threat of the first snowfall to finally get rid of those pesky, binocular-wielding tormentors and their equally annoying offspring.

36

TAKE A HIKE!

CLIMBING IN the Canadian Rockies can be quite painful. No, I'm not registering displeasure. I'm merely pointing out what Suzanne and I did today—not once but three times!!! Ouch! My poor, aching feet, not to mention my voluptuous, well-nourished body, already battered by another forced march through hell less than 24 hours earlier.

Let's be honest now. Have you ever been in a situation where the only thing that keeps you going is pride? You know the feeling. Every fiber of your body is crying out for relief and begging you for an end to this physical torture. But pride, stubborn pride, will just not let you give in, even given the seemingly insurmountable odds.

This ordeal brought to mind, all too vividly, a similar event that took place a long time ago in Ethiopia. We had gone to a campsite at the bottom of a deep canyon not far from the capital city of Addis Ababa. Instead of enjoying the accomplishment, I spent the entire weekend staring up at the only way out—a perpendicular wall of rock that seemed to get steeper by the minute.

Eventually the climb out could be delayed no longer, even though I did give serious thought of abandoning my journalism career and staying there permanently. But climb out I did, swearing and sweating all the way up in a vain search for inspiration and strength.

Well, it was just about that same scenario (at least for this ole geezer) when we decided to stroll up to a place called Parker Ridge, just one of a seemingly endless number of fabulous lookouts scattered throughout Jasper National Park in the Canadian Rockies. Let me read you the come-on from the tourist brochure. "A short but steep trail—820 feet elevation gain, 1.5 miles return—ends with a great view of the Saskatchewan Glacier."

Suzanne capturing some of the beauty of the Canadian Rockies.

So what's there to worry about, right? After all, my trusting nature assured me that if this trail were only fit for mountain goats, chamois or other cliff clingers, then they certainly would have said so. My trusting nature aside, it still would have been reassuring for the blurb to have included one of those "degree of difficulty" labels, if for no other reason than for that extra peace of mind.

There were also no instructions about clothing to wear, such as wind breakers, wool caps (an especially important fact for us hair-challenged folks), etc. Since it was midsummer, I must confess that "minor" omission got lost in the shuffle and anticipation of what lay at the end of the climb. But very soon into our walk it became painfully evident that around these parts altitude does indeed influence attitude.

As we began our ascent up and up past the tree line, then through the tundra, only to be assaulted by gale force winds and biting cold, I must admit my attitude began matching the bleakness of the terrain. If the truth be known, if I could have done it with good grace (and without anyone seeing me) I would have done one of these quick about faces and faked a successful summit assault.

But I was all too aware I'd never be allowed to live down that piece of lazy chicanery with Suzanne, who was not only setting a hot and heavy pace, but also keeping a wary eye on the sluggard bringing up the rear. Somehow, some way, I managed to haul this ole carcass to the top. How it happened is still a mystery to me.

And, yet again, we were being treated to that all-too-familiar reward of sensory overload, with snow-capped peaks and glaciers thrown in for good measure. You can tell I'm getting frustrated at having to come up with new and unique words to describe all this beauty we're experiencing along the way.

Maybe it's time for yours truly to come up with my very own vocabulary of scenic words and expressions—all brand spanking new, shiny and unique—to express my feelings about all the beauty that millions before us have also struggled to describe in new, creative and non-cliched ways. But please don't hold your breath on that one.

Serendipities occur when you least expect them. I guess that's why they're called serendipities. On the way back down

I met some good folks from Australia, the country of my birth more years ago than I'd like to recall. Of course, I immediately twigged their accent and before you knew it we were speaking "straiin" about my home town of Tarragindi and the Boomerang movie theater in nearby Annerley, where I used to go every Saturday to see my two full-length features, a bunch of Tom and Jerry cartoons and a serial featuring Tom Mix, Hopalong Cassidy or some other western hero.

Before we parted, one of our new Aussie friends suggested I get a book written about life in Tarragindi and environs in the 1950s, the exact time when I was growing up there. Can't wait to get on the Internet and track it down. What a great bunch of friendly folks. I didn't have the heart to tell them that they weren't even half way up to the summit, as some of them looked done in already!

Earlier in the day we had limbered up by taking a short but steep climb (are there any other kind in this area?) up to Jasper National Park's Columbia Icefields and got up close and personal with a glacier that's making a fast retreat.

The case for dramatic climate change was made compellingly on the drive up to the glacier from the parking lot. Every so often, marker signs indicated the location of the glacier year after year since 1950, when it began its rapid retreat. As if to add an exclamation point to it all, I overheard one guide quoting experts as saying this particular glacier won't even exist in 30 years. Now that's an attention getter!

I must be turning into an old grouch. But for the life of me I can't figure out why people insist on ignoring the warning signs not to walk on the glacier. It's not as if there's no danger involved. What we're talking about here are crevasses 12 stories deep that folks have fallen into and died. But it always happens to the other guy, right?

A lovely, short, undemanding walk wrapped up an equally

short driving day along the Icefields Parkway into neighboring Banff National Park. That led us down to the Mistaya Canyon, the Mistaya River's handiwork of more than 10,000 years. Talk about the relentless power of water.

Our home base was a beautiful little campground (31 sites) called Waterfowl Campground. It's surrounded by snowcapped peaks (what else, in this country!) and featuring a lovely emerald green lake at one end.

Our last night there it rained. No matter because it was fascinating nonetheless sitting in our camper watching the snow accumulate on the sides of mountains just a few hundred feet higher up. The summer season was surely winding down but no worries, as our Bigfoot truck camper's thick insulation means nights inside are warm and toasty.

But clearly the time for more walks, strenuous or not, was at an end. And for my tired old body that came not a moment too soon, even though I'd be the last to admit it in public. However, winter walks on some pristine beach on Mexico's Baja Peninsula or somewhere else nice and warm are another matter entirely. It's amazing, the motivational powers of a little warmth.

37

I'M BUSHED!

No, I'm not getting political on you! In fact, the condition I'm in, I'd be hard pressed to give you any party affiliation.

Let me put it another way by borrowing a saying from my late Australian mother: "I'm so out of it, I can't tell whether I'm Arthur or Martha!" Now when you get to that point, my friend, let me assure you that you've got big, big troubles!

If you haven't already guessed, I'm referring to my physical state or the total lack thereof! How do I put it more succinctly? I'm gonzo, je suis tres fatigue, I'm akin to a slab of dead meat, not to mention being totally exhausted. All right, let's not beat a dead horse. I think you get the picture.

You've probably noticed that I'm being very careful not to lump Suzanne's physical condition in with mine. A wag once described his wife as "part mountain goat but without the beard." I wouldn't go that far because I enjoy living. Rather, employing classic understatement, I'd venture to say that my wife's in slightly better physical condition than this, dare I say, rather chubby specimen. Now doesn't the euphemistic chubby sound better than fat or even overweight?

Unbeknownst to me, my physical deterioration started innocently enough as we left Jasper heading west, northwest along

Highway 16, known throughout Canada as the Yellowhead. Our destination was British Columbia's Mt. Robson Provincial Park, home to the Canadian Rockies' highest peak at more than 13,000 feet.

More specifically, we were hoping to catch a glimpse of that park's crown jewel, named after the first non-Indian chap to "discover" it. I use the word "hoping" advisedly because, as we'd ruefully learned previously, these mountains, especially the higher ones, love to play hide and seek with the tourists. It's as if they delight in frustrating the bussed-in set during their "It's-Tuesday,-so-it-must-be-Mt.-Robson" type of holidays!

On paper, no one could be faulted if this mere "provincial park" were given a miss. After all, what's another mountain, no matter how majestic and beautiful, after your senses have been steadily bombarded by the seemingly endless chain of the peaks that help make up this most spectacular area known as the Canadian Rockies.

In fact, we almost gave Mt. Robson a miss ourselves. That was before we compared notes with some fellow RVers who described it as a "must see."

Right there and then we were sold, because in RVer parlance, a "must see" represents the very highest rating that can be bestowed on a tourist attraction. I'll let you in on the intricacies of this hitherto top-secret rating system. It all starts with the "don't bother," then moves higher past "if you have time," to eventually end with the rave "must see," with countless nuanced stops in between.

Not wanting to tire ourselves out on preliminaries, we naturally drove up as far as we were allowed to the base camp. There we began what a sign described as a "leisurely walk to Lake Kinney" at the foot of this mighty massif.

An hour and a half and two and a half miles later (we weren't exactly breaking any records for speed) we arrived at the lake, having ascended countless hundreds of feet. Wow, was the effort ever worth it! In fact, the scene before us represented one of those times where reality truly outdoes the most flattering of postcards.

On our right was Mt. Robson, its crown bathed in white from nearly year-round snows plus the seemingly ever-present clouds and glaciers. Forming the rest of the mountainous amphitheater were equally impressive peaks, while in the foreground lay Lake Kinney, a greenish-blue dazzler, glinting in the sun. It was truly a sight to behold, to trot out that old tried but true tourist cliché. I'll try to work in "wish you were here" a little later!

I can't recall how long we sat there soaking it all in with eye and camera. But slowly but surely the harsh reality of Newton's "what goes up, must come down" began to sink in. Thinking back on it, I must have known I was a hurting puppy because, for an instant, just a fleeting instant, I contemplated braving the elements and spending the night right where I sat.

But spurred on by the image of becoming bait for wolf, bear or coyote, I staggered to my feet and headed down the trail, with Suzanne setting her usual demanding pace up ahead. True to form, it only took us about half the time to descend. But at what price! By the time we reached "base camp" my legs felt like piano strings immediately following a Bach Cantata, still quivering mightily from the onslaught of lactic acid buildup.

We debated staying in one of the two campgrounds located nearer the base of Mt. Robson in the hopes that the morning would afford us a better view of the elusive peak. But we decided against it and drove the 40 miles back along the Yellowhead to the same campground in Jasper where we had stayed the night before.

And are we glad we did. Get this. The night before tackling Mt. Robson we had the place virtually to ourselves, a perfect situation for spotting elk, so we were told.

Talk about the kiss of death. I wish folks, well-meaning or not, would stop dispensing such local folklore, which, for us at least, almost never seems to prove accurate. Having said that, you know what's coming next? You got it, not an elk within a 1,000 miles was my guess.

Well, that night we returned from our Mt. Robson experience to find the place packed to the gills with RVs of every size, shape and description. I mean it was chock-a-block from one end to the other! So what happens? That's right. A big bull elk and his harem of six or seven cows come wandering nonchalantly through the center of our mini-city, to the delight of all.

Now there are bull elk and there are BULL ELK! You should have seen this dude. Not only was he huge and, for all appearances, in his prime, but he had a rack of antlers on him that would have made Ernest Hemingway weep with admiration. The only word that describes them is majestic. And this particular bull elk seemed to know he was the main man as well.

He couldn't give a hoot about us. His main concern seemed to be keeping would-be suitors away from his women. And, to this end, he regularly sounded the challenge, just in case these lurking lotharios had any ideas of horning in...or should I say "antlering" in!

What I wouldn't have given to have my professional grade tape recorder at the ready to capture his aggressive sounds for posterity. It's one of those almost eerie calls that defy description. It's like the fellow says, you had to have been there.

Giving it my best shot, I'd say it combined elements of a hacking cough and a strong lusty bellow, which, in Elk-speak, must have sounded mighty powerful and impressive indeed.

And what a fitting end to our all-too-brief tour of the Canadian Rockies. I can see why the world raves about this most impressive mountain range, straddling the provinces of British Columbia and Alberta.

There's no denying that the scenery is superb. And possibly therein lies the great danger. It's apparent that many of the man-made trappings that accompany such scenic wonders threaten to "kill them with kindness."

One hardly has to look beyond many of the towns that have surrendered their original charm to the honky tonk, trivial and oft-times vulgar. I sometimes despair that, for the sake of the almighty Canadian one dollar coin, the loonie, there are those who, if allowed, would gladly risk marring forever the very scenery that attracts folks there in the first place.

And add overcrowded, noisy campgrounds to the "joys" of traveling during the height of the tourist season, rather than "on the shoulders" as is generally our wont. For the uninitiated, "on the shoulders" means those times of the year just before or after the peak tourist season when things are decidedly quieter but also when the weather is potentially less than ideal.

But let's not get too self-centered here. Not everyone has the luxury of picking and choosing when they can visit a certain tourist attraction. For the younger generation, there are school holidays to be considered: for adults, work vacations that can only be taken at certain times of the year and countless other circumstances. Hence, the summertime crush.

Also, the further north one travels, the less "on the shoulders" leeway there is. Locals tell us that up in these parts it can go from summer and autumn to winter in the matter of a few weeks. So unless your rig is well insulated and you enjoy snow camping, it's best to be ready to be one of those countless RV snowbirds flying due south in search of much warmer climes.

But thankfully those first snows are still several weeks away. So the good folks in places like Florida, Mexico, Texas, the American Southwest and the like will have to wait a spell before seeing a flood of Maughan dollars down there. For now, we're more than content spending our fair share of loonies and twonies north of the border, as long as our wallets and my old legs hold up!

38

CYPRESS HILLS BLUES

CAMPED HERE by Lake Elkwater in bucolic Cypress Hills Inter Provincial Park, which straddles the Canadian provinces of Alberta and Saskatchewan, the world's woes seemed so far away. Just a few hours earlier, we had driven in from the city of Medicine Hat across dry and dusty prairies.

Even though we had checked and rechecked our map, the seemingly endless flatness continued to stretch out before us. Could we have made a mistake? Or was it just our befuddled state of mind?

Then looming in the distance we began to see the first far-off glimpses of lovely, verdant hills covered with what turned out to be spruce, aspen and various species of evergreens. As we got even closer, this shimmering mirage turned out to be an oasis of sorts, surrounded by all the summer dryness of southern Alberta.

In point of fact, it turned out that we were only 25 miles from the border with Montana, a geographic fact quite comforting, given that the date was September 12, 2001. For all too obvious reasons, I recall searching the radio dial until finding a station broadcasting out of Great Falls, Montana.

Better, we thought, to have Americans trying to explain the insanity of the previous day than Canadians. Though in all fairness, we had found Canadian coverage of that Tuesday's terrorist attacks thorough and remarkably insightful. Still and all, this was a time for brother to talk to brother and sister to sister.

Talk about mixed emotions. We wanted more news, but in other ways we didn't. It's like the analogy of the moth and the flame. Like all Americans, we were hurting physically and mentally, but nonetheless through the pain we were somehow still searching for something to make sense of it all. It was as if we were saying: "Give me the silver bullet to take all the pain away!"

Although we had obviously driven into Cypress Hills Inter-Provincial Park, mentally we had, in fact, staggered in. Upon reflection, Calgary and Medicine Hat seemed like a blur. We functioned while there—but not really, if you know what I mean. It's amazing that we managed to avoid a major accident, zoned out as we obviously were.

Let me try to explain it this way. Way back when Suzanne and I were sparking and courting I splurged and took her to a foreign cinema house to see a French avant-garde film called *Last Year at Marienbad*.

I remember not caring for the film at the time, even though I managed to disguise my total lack of understanding and inter-est very well. But, on a subconscious level, that rather bizarre film must have made a lasting impression on me because, to this day, I recall how the entire cast moved through the movie in slow motion, as in some sort of dream or trance.

At long last, we now felt we were beginning to understand the feeling the director was trying to convey with that rather audacious cinematic technique. But understanding was one thing. Truly coming to grips with the events of 9/11 was another matter entirely.

One thing was clear to us: we'd have to get it together again mentally if we weren't just to waste time and diesel fuel wandering around aimlessly, looking but not really seeing. We honestly didn't know how long it would take us to get our feet back under us again. But if we were ever to accomplish this healing, Cypress Hills was the perfect place to start.

First off, we had to purge ourselves of the notion that we no longer had the right to be enjoying ourselves when so many of our fellow Americans had been killed or injured. Earlier, this guilt had manifested itself when we deliberately passed up a visit to Alberta's Dinosaur Provincial Park, which, in normal times, would have been a must-see.

Cypress Hills has a different, somewhat less demanding, feel to it—a feel that lends itself to whatever mood you bring to the place. If you want to play very vigorously you've come to the right place. It's got it all—from golf to bike rentals, swimming and much more. On the other hand, if you want a place of quiet contemplation, then there's that in abundance as well. We wanted the latter and all the park could offer.

I can't quite remember how many days we languished there, sleeping, snacking, listening to the news, even shedding tears. What I do recall, however, is the feeling of utter tranquility slowly but surely replenishing our mental equilibrium. To use the vernacular, we were getting it back together. And soon we'd be ready to reclaim our lives as full-time RVers and not just aimlessly wandering automatons.

As this steadiness of purpose returned, so did my resolve to reach out via email to our many friends and relatives around the world. They had written of their concern for us personally and for our country in general in the wake of 9/11. And we found this show of heartfelt concern most comforting indeed.

Feeding off my newfound strength, I sought to reassure

them through the thoughts of Abraham Lincoln that we all would be happy again, even though right now that fact might not seem possible. And as Lincoln summed up his thoughts: "Knowing this, and truly believing that to be the case, would make us less miserable now."

It wasn't long thereafter that we were out and about sampling a lot of what Cypress Hills had to offer. Fort Walsh National Historic Site proved worthwhile, as did the Visitor Centre, with its excellent overview of the park's abundant flora and fauna.

But it was the non-structured part of the park that ultimately proved the most beneficial. Here we could amble along the Beaver Creek Trail System, choosing those along the shoreline of Lake Elkwater or other, slightly more demanding, ones leading into nearby hills.

Cypress Hills proved just the tonic we needed. Soon the idea of not only returning to the road, but actually enjoying the experience, began to make sense once again.

It's strange how people or places are put in your life for some unfathomable reason. Cypress Hills will always be such a place for us. It became our refuge, our place to hunker down and pick up our mental pieces. We can only hope that other folks found their own versions of Cypress Hills and the peace and tranquility to make sense of their lives as well.

If the events of September 11, 2001, taught us one thing, it was how interconnected we all are, whether we want to admit it or not.

EPILOGUE

WHILE EVERY effort has been made to be as factual and current as possible, more than eight years have passed since our trip to the Pacific Northwest. Situations change, such as the death in 2006 of Gold Rush pioneer, Harrie Hughes, the inspiration for the chapter entitled, "Been There, Done That."

But, for the most part, change here comes slowly, even grudgingly, and then only in concert with the indomitable will and fiercely independent spirit of the inhabitants of this part of North America. And that remains as implacable as ever.